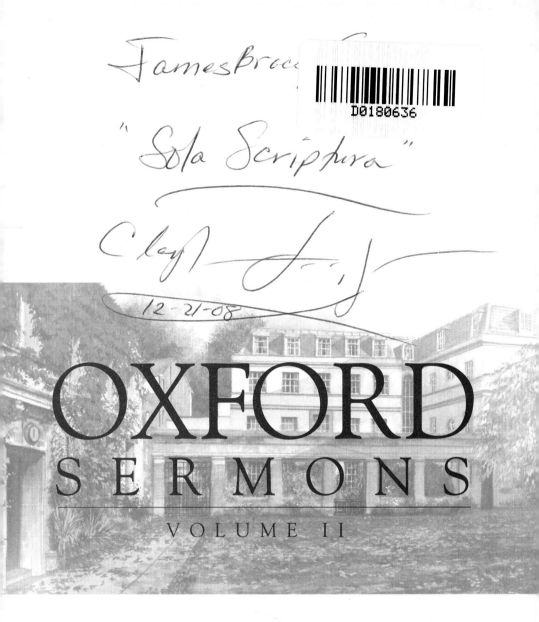

James Broc...

" Sola Scriptura "

Clay ...

12-21-08

OXFORD
SERMONS

VOLUME II

HUPOMONE PRESS
FORT WORTH, TEXAS

Library of Congress Cataloging-in-Publication Data

Oxford Sermons 2008/Dr. Joel C. Gregory, gen. ed., 1948-

Includes index.

ISBN: 978-1-60725-373-0

DEDICATION

TO DR. WILLIAM CROUCH
PRESIDENT
GEORGETOWN COLLEGE

The visionary leader whose leadership
opened the door to Oxford

PREFACE

It was on a 2004 pre-dawn ride to the airport through the bluegrass horse farms between Georgetown and Lexington. Georgetown College president William Crouch had asked to take me to the airport. I had spoken at the college pastors' conference. Dr. Crouch had an intuitive hunch that we had some things in common to discuss. We did. We revealed our mutual interests in ministerial training, diversity in educa-tion and racial reconciliation. He wanted to risk something bold at Georgetown, the oldest Baptist institution west of the Alleghenies, with roots back to 1787. I had a dream to honor the late Rev. Dr. E. K. Bailey, who opened doors for me. There was also a desire to help preachers grow as proclaimers with intense, interactive small seminars tailored for those attending.

Dr. Crouch and I both agree that this was an eventful drive in the dark through the white double fences of the manicured thoroughbred farms. That conversation led to the birth of an effort to revive on the campus of Georgetown the spirit of Bishop College, the historic black college that closed in Dallas in 1988. Doors opened across America for Bill to present that vision to conferences, conventions and individual congregations. That vision evolved into a larger effort to embrace the sons and daughters of Bishop College graduates as Bishop Legacy Graduates of Georgetown. All of this is unfolding even now and will cut a path in American higher education never traveled before.

Another component of that airport ride-vision emerged as Proclaimers Place. Years before this, I read that the Bishop of Durham,

B.F. Westcott, met weekly with his parish priests to discuss the lectionary text for the next Sunday. He combined exegesis and homiletics in a small-group discussion. For years I had wanted to do that with and for working pastors. Bill and I conceived the concept of Proclaimers Place, a four-day seminar for a small group of pastors working on one text per day and moving from text to sermon. The seminar combines close exegetical work with a variety of suggestions for shaping that exegesis into a biblical sermon. The pedagogy of the seminar evokes principles for homiletics from the study of specific texts.

Since the inception of Proclaimers Place in 2005, there have been 33 seminars held in 15 states along with Regents Park College, Oxford, involving 211 preachers. What began as a dream on an airport drive has become a significant movement.

The most surprising feature of Proclaimers Place has been the participation in the summer sessions at Regents Park College, Oxford. Dr. Crouch, a trustee of that Baptist college affiliated with Oxford University, enabled a relationship with Regents Park for Proclaimers Place. Former Regents Park principal Paul Fiddes and the current principal Rob Ellis have warmly embraced the program for four years. In 2005 there were 11 participants in one week. We changed the format from one to two sessions, four days each, in 2006-2008. We have had 43, 27 and 39 participants, respectively, over those three years for a total attendance of 120 during the four-year span the seminar has been held. In 2008 we added a final day for touring historic preaching sites in London.

Baptist World Alliance president David Coffee has attended the seminar and has adopted its methodology in order to present similar seminars among British Baptists.

For the second time, participants in the seminar indicated their desire to produce an anthology of sermons. This volume, the second of its kind, presents sermons by 22 participants. Many of these messages are based on common elements and principles discussed in the seminar. They also represent the freedom, individuality and personality of the various proclaimers involved. The contributors have applied some of the principles discussed at Oxford to a wide variety of biblical texts and approaches to crafting sermons. I have acted as a general editor of this collection while giving full freedom to the style and voice of the participants. The result is a volume of lively, relevant, biblical sermons stamped with the authority of the text and the personalities of the individual preachers.

The publisher presents this book as a glimpse of a moment caught in time—a memorable few days spent by these preachers at one of the earth's most venerated centers of education, focusing on the endless challenge of speaking God's Word to each generation.

—Joel C. Gregory
Distinguished Fellow
Georgetown College
Professor of Preaching
George W. Truett Theological Seminary
Baylor University

CONTENTS

There's a Bright Side Somewhere
(1 Peter 5:10,11)

PASTOR LAWRENCE E. AKER III

Cornerstone Baptist Church
Brooklyn, New York

There is an intriguing legend concerning the Franciscans. According to Bruce Thieleman, they were the first ones to grow grapes systematically in California. They grew the Muscat grapes used to make Muscatel wine. One year they suffered through a horrible drought, and all the grapes withered on the vine. They thought they were going to lose them all, but they took those grapes down into the towns and sold them as what they called "Peruvian delicacies." This was the beginning of the California Associated Raisin Company, known today as the Sun-Maid Raisin Company.

The Franciscans were able to find hope in the midst of an agricultural disaster. Likewise, in our passage the apostle Peter wrote to scattered Jewish Christians facing a political disaster. Under the leadership of Nero, the Roman Empire sought to persecute, abuse and ultimately eliminate all Christians. In spite of this persecution, Peter penned his epistle to give faith, comfort and hope to believers.

Peter's aim is to put into perspective the eternal hope that we have in our resurrected Lord Jesus Christ. As followers of Christ, we will undoubtedly suffer for our faith. Ian Maclaren, a Scottish theologian, once mused, "The highest joy to the Christian almost always comes through suffering. No flower can bloom in paradise which is not transplanted from Gethsemane." Regardless of how or where we see suffering, whether it be Wall Street woes, hurricane displacement, international wars or personal disappointments, one relevant question remains: How do we gather the dried vines of life and turn them into sweet raisins of hope? Is it possible to find a bright side in life?

We can find assurance from the apostle Peter, knowing that *The Crises That We Face in Life Are Temporary*, but *The Comfort That God Gives Is*

Timeless. Therefore, *We See God in His Complete Totality* carrying us through the most difficult and trying situations of life.

THE CRISES THAT WE FACE IN LIFE ARE TEMPORARY

Peter asserts, "After you have suffered for a little while…" The readers may have wondered, "How long is a little while?" In 1 Peter 1:6, the apostle reminds us that our trials are only "for a season."

There is a French proverb which states, "Misfortune rides in on horseback, and it walks out on two feet." This statement underscores the swiftness with which trials can come our way and their longevity until departure. In the course of our lives,

* Sickness can ride into our lives at the most inopportune moment.
* Financial obstacles can ride into our lives.
* Losing a loved one can ride into our lives.
* Family concerns can ride into our lives.
* Unexpected scenarios can ride into our lives.

Yet, these are the crisis points which are all temporary in the grand plans of our omnipotent God. Even though they may be uncomfortable and unwanted, they are needed to conform us into the image of Christ.

While I was in graduate school, my wife worked for a season with a temporary agency. It was a time that required flexibility on her part. She would normally receive different assignments regularly. Some of the jobs had great ambience and staff. A few times the assignments were lackluster and unfulfilling. However, the bright side was that we always knew they were temporary assignments.

Everything that we encounter in life comes directly from the Heavenly Father, our divine personnel agent. He places us in different temporary situations: Some of them are positive experiences, and some are not. Nevertheless, He knows when to remove us from our temporary assignments in life. Peter wanted to encourage Christians throughout the provinces of Pontus, Galatia, Cappadocia, Asia and Bithynia that what they were facing hadn't escaped God. Author Warren Wiersbe notes that when God permits His children to go through the furnace, He keeps His eye on the clock and His hand on the thermostat.

THE COMFORT THAT GOD GIVES IS TIMELESS

Peter says, "After you have suffered for a little while, the *God of all grace* who called you into His eternal glory by Christ Jesus, perfect, establish, and strengthen you." Hence, the contrast is *suffering* for a little while, compared to a glory that is *eternal*.

The God of all grace can make the difficulties that we encounter in this life bearable. The designation is a close synonym to the Pauline reference in 1 Corinthians 1:3: "the God of all comfort." Notice the Petrine emphasis in the phrase, "the God of *all* grace." The definite modifier *all* enlarges the meaning of how God's grace meets human need. In the backdrop of persecution, first-century Christians could find solace in God's manifold care. We also, through the lenses of 21st-century faith, can claim this same assurance. God has provided all that is needed to sustain His children. F.B. Meyer defined God's multifaceted ways as, "Illuminating grace for the seeker; justifying grace for the believer; comforting grace for the bereaved and sorrowful; strengthening grace for the weak and downtrodden; sanctifying grace for the unholy; living grace and dying grace."

During the 2008 Olympic Games in Beijing, Michael Phelps turned in an incredible performance. On his way to eight gold medals, he persevered through fatigue, mental stress and even equipment failure. Phelps experienced a goggles gaffe. While competing in the 200-meter butterfly, his goggles filled up with water, so his sight was obstructed by tiny bubbles. Phelps would later tell reporters that he could not see anything for the last 100 meters. So how did he win while chlorine burned and blinded his eyes?

While in training, his coach Bob Bowman showed Phelps how to count his strokes while in competition. This allowed him to stay on pace, despite his adversity. Perhaps Phelps could endure because he realized the future glory of yet another gold medal was greater than the temporary discomfort that besieged him.

Likewise, our heavenly coach Jesus Christ encourages us to continue to stroke ahead, regardless of what we face. He says, "In this life you will have trials and tribulations, but be of good cheer for I have overcome the world" (John 16:33).

Peter wants us to see that what we face on earth cannot be compared to what awaits us in glory. The apostle Paul said in Romans 8:18: "For I consider that the sufferings of this present time are not worthy to be compared with the glory that is to be revealed to us."

We can have confidence in knowing that God's grace is sufficient for every type of situation in life. Hindus would say our trials are bad karma, while Confucius would claim that we have failed to learn from mistakes of the past. For the Christian, however, suffering is just a necessary path that leads to future glory. This is a timeless comfort which endures forever.

WE SEE GOD IN HIS COMPLETE TOTALITY

God is completely involved with our circumstances. Peter the fisherman fuses together four verbs to reinforce the point that God is able to sustain us. The nuances of the verbs describe God's protective care. Scholars suggest that they are designed as a literary device to show God's all-sufficiency.

He says God will *perfect* us. In the original language, the word is *kartizo*, which means "to carefully mend," similar to how a fisherman would have to mend a fish net. Another meaning of the word is "to restore to its former condition." Our God is able to mend and repair our lives, regardless of what we face. God will make us adequate to face whatever difficulties lie ahead.

God will also *establish* us, in order to keep us steadfast and firm. The promise in 2 Thessalonians 3:3 is a natural parallel: "The Lord is faithful who shall establish you, and preserve you from evil." Here, it means to be fixed in faith without vacillation.

Although Peter had once denied Christ, he was now standing firm to proclaim God's power.

But also, God will *strengthen* us. This is a reference to an inner strength to combat outward circumstances. Similarly the apostle Paul prayed in Ephesians 3:16 that "believers might have strength in the inner man (being)."

Finally, God will *settle* us. The word refers to "that which is made to rest securely, to lay the foundation of." In the Sermon on the Mount, Jesus contrasted the wise and the foolish builder. The wise builder created a firm (settled) foundation before building his home. Therefore, when the storms and wind came, it did not fall. The other built "upon sand." When the windstorms came, it fell.

The eminent New Testament scholar J.A. Bengal translates this verse, "God shall perfect, that no defect remain in you, shall establish that nothing may shake you, shall strengthen that you may overcome every adverse force."

Peter piles together four future indicatives to describe the totality of an all-encompassing God. What assurance we are given as we face the hardships of life! The Prince of Preachers, C. H. Spurgeon, once said, "There are no crown-wearers in heaven who were not cross-bearers here below." We do not face anything that saints before us have not already endured.

Peter begins his letter with a message of encouragement to beleaguered Christians. He reminds us that we have a living hope (1:3). It is this hope that allows us to prevail through the vicissitudes of life. Rev. Ted DeHass has noted that Alaska has a beautiful flower known as the fireweed, which epitomizes the believer's journey. This multifaceted blossom can easily be termed as good for whatever ails you. It can be used as soothing salve for insect bites, cuts and eczema. It can also be used as a tea remedy for coughs, asthma and upset stomachs. These unique blossoms are also used to make tasty honey or jelly.

However, the delicate, purple-pink blossoms only come out after some heat. Fireweed derives its name because it is the first plant to bloom after a fire. In the aftermath, when the smoke clears and the earth cools, the fireweed emerges from the blackened earth. Fireweed then blankets the landscape like a beautiful quilt.

There is a bright side to our dilemmas in life. Just as God allows fireweed to bloom, He also calls us to bloom in the aftermath of our fiery trials. To Him be glory, forever and ever, Amen.

Storms
(Mark 4:35-41)

⁓⊱❈⊰⁓

REV. DR. T. O'BRIAN BERRY
*Greater True Light Missionary Baptist Church
Houston, Texas*

I normally volunteer for the Oak Village Middle School every so often, just to be an outlet for their students and staff. This neighborhood middle school is not only the school I have adopted, but it is also the one I attended in the early '80s. So there is a sense of pride there for me as I walk those halls and frequent the classrooms.

But this one particular morning was altogether different from any average morning. I was assisting with the showers of some adults from our neighboring state of Louisiana. The Red Cross had set up a shelter in Thurgood Marshall Elementary School, behind the church I serve as the senior pastor—Greater True Light Missionary Baptist Church in Houston, Texas. There were about 200 people from New Orleans living there because of the devastation left by Hurricane Katrina in late August of 2005.

Thurgood Marshall served as a great place for a shelter, but it did not have any showers to service the already disenfranchised who were there temporarily. So as part of an agreement between the North Forest Independent School District and the Red Cross on behalf of the evacuees, there had to be supervision for them to shower at Oak Village. Our church and several other congregations in our community pledged that we would assist the shelter at night with the showering. So as providence would have it, I was part of the volunteer group for that morning.

Now, I love people. I have been called to serve people. But the news of the morning just took some life out of me. Hurricane Rita was heading our way. We were still dealing with the aftereffects of Katrina, and now Rita was at our doorstep. I thought to myself, "We don't need another storm. What's with all these storms coming our way? We really can do without this type of activity. God, why another storm?"

GOD, WHY ANOTHER STORM?

Many people asked that question during that time regarding the physical storms, but have you ever asked that question in your spiritual walk? "God, why another storm? I am having too many issues in my life. I just finished getting over a long-term illness, and now my marriage is on the rocks. My child just graduated and wants to go to college, but they say I make too much money for her to get financial aid. Too much money! Whose bank account are they looking at? (I thank God for free checking. A certain amount doesn't have to be there to keep it open.) My insurance requires me to pay a major deductible up front. I am really sick, but I can't miss work. God forbid, my prescription deductible has not been fulfilled. I really can do without these circumstances at this time. God, why another storm? Couldn't I just have a few days of peace?"

Storms, regardless of what you name them, come for different reasons. I believe some storms are meant to direct us to the right path, as it was with Jonah, the minor prophet. Others happen because we disobey the man of God, as with those on the ship with the apostle Paul in Acts 27. Furthermore, I believe that there is at least one more reason why God uses storms. God uses storms to develop us spiritually. He did this for the disciples in Mark 4:35-41. This storm was intended to assist with their development.

Mark 4 begins with Jesus using parables to teach the disciples about Himself. He expresses and explains this purpose privately to them. If anyone needed to know who He was, it would be those whom He would initially entrust the care of the church to. They did not understand it on the shore and in the boat, so He moves them out on the sea in the boat.

Some students just need a change of scenery or no scenery at all to benefit from the information taught. On many days in my classes, when a student would act up in the back of the class, the teacher automatically moved him/her to the front. Not much space or many chairs between the teacher and student left very little room for distractions. Jesus, being the Master Teacher, says to His church leaders in training: "Let us go over to the other side. While we are going, I will allow the scenery to change for My glory and your development." This journey would develop them in many ways.

STORMS RESULT IN SOCIAL DEVELOPMENT

He first develops them socially, *away from the masses*. The Scripture plainly says that they left the multitude behind. Many may want to travel with you to the other side, but few are fit for the journey to go with you. We have no issues with our foes being left behind. There will be some who are friends that will be disqualified. I even will go so far to say that there will be some family members staying while you are sailing. Regardless of their status in our lives, the truth still is that many will have to be left. They will want to go, but they have to be left. There rarely will be any volunteers to stay. You just have to leave some people behind. They are developed socially, *alone with the Master*. There is no time like quality time alone with the Master—no interruptions or unnecessary outbursts. The Creator just spends private time with His creation. The Master is developing His masterpiece.

THE "SHIPS" OF SPIRITUAL DEVELOPMENT

Second, He develops them with the *ships* that follow Him. The King James Version plainly says that there were other little ships that followed the Lord's boat. It was not strange for ships to follow Christ, because follow-ship, fellowship, stewardship, discipleship and lordship all come along with Christ Jesus:

- *Follow-ship*—"Follow me as I follow Christ" (1 Cor. 11:1).
- *Fellowship*—"And when the day of Pentecost was fully come, they were all with one accord in one place" (Acts 2:1).
- *Discipleship*—"Take my yoke upon you, and learn of me; for I am meek and lowly in heart: and ye shall find rest unto your souls. For my yoke is easy, and my burden is light" (Matt. 11:29-30).
- *Stewardship*—"Moreover it is required in stewards, that a man be found faithful" (1 Cor. 4:2).

The pinnacle ship that I believe the Lord would have us to reach is:

- *Lordship*— "And that every tongue should confess that Jesus Christ is Lord, to the glory of God the Father" (Phil. 2:11).

All of these ships are essential for our spiritual development. I just believe that the Lord's ultimate plan is that we reach lordship. When Jesus is our Lord, we have no problem following Him in fellowship with other disciples as stewards of each other at the command of the Lord. Yes, He was developing them with the ships that followed.

WHEN GOD ANSWERS WITH SILENCE

The third area of their development was with silence. Never shall I forget my seventh-grade reading teacher. She kept our undivided attention with a commanding voice. She was the teacher whom you heard before you saw. Even today I can't tell which was the most effective— her tone or her technique. We learned the lesson, but I can't say it wasn't our fear that her loud voice would embarrass us. Jesus, while on this boat, wasn't loud in His efforts to develop them. As a matter of fact, for much of the journey He was asleep.

Have you ever felt like Jesus was asleep while you were in your storm? I know the Bible records that He never sleeps nor slumbers as God. But have you ever been in a situation where you had to ask the Lord, "Where are You? I need to (or can I) hear from You?" By all indications you were tempted to label His state as one of being asleep. These disciples give us insight that even if it appears that He is asleep, He will get up at a disciple's request. When they wake Him, He works on them with silence. He gets up, but says nothing to them.

Likewise, when you call on Jesus, I know you expect to hear from Him. But here is the truth. There are several ways the Lord will answer us. He will either say yes, no, wait or nothing. Yes, sometimes He will answer you with silence. In the second chapter of Jonah, the prophet prays to God but receives no answer. However, God did speak to the fish. Elijah on Mt. Carmel prays for rain seven times but receives no answer for him or his servant. But God speaks to the clouds. Sometimes He doesn't have to speak to you; on the contrary, it is often your situation that needs to be spoken to. It is the same with these disciples. Though He says nothing to them, He does speak to the wind and the waves that were affecting them. He majors in working on the other end. I believe He doesn't initially speak to them because of the content of what He is going to say. Notice what Mark 4:40 says, "And He said unto them, Why are ye so fearful? How is it that ye have no faith?" If He asks these questions while the wind and waves are still raging, it could have been emotionally traumatic for the disciples. My mother says all the time, "If you don't have anything good to say, don't say anything." So, for a time Jesus develops them with silence.

Finally, I believe that He uses this storm to develop them to see the Son and not the storm, or more specifically, the Son in the storm—not merely just the son of Mary and Joseph, but God the Son. They come away from this miracle still clueless regarding the identity of Jesus. Their final question to each other is, "What manner of man is this that even the winds and the waves obey him?" He is not just a *man*. He is God the Son. Somebody should have come to that conclusion.

"LORD" IS THE MAGIC WORD

But being a merciful God, He gives them another storm to get it right. In contrast to this storm, two chapters later He dismisses them to go across the lake without Him. Mark's Gospel does not give us all the details of their communication, but Matthew does. He says that while they were in this storm without Jesus, He comes, even without them, calling to Him. When they see Him this time, they address Him rightly. They don't refer to Him as a man. Peter, the spokesman of the group, says, "Lord. . ." There is something about calling Him Lord. When he says, "Lord," he even gets to walk on the water while the tempest is raging. Yes, when you know Him as Lord, you can have peace in the midst of the storm. Yes, when you know Him as Lord, nature doesn't have to be normal or natural for you to do the supernatural. "Lord" has to be the magic word.

I shall never forget Captain Marvel. Captain Marvel is a superhero featured in a "fictional character" comic book originally published by Fawcett Comics, now owned by DC Comics. Created in 1939 by artist C. C. Beck and writer Bill Parker, the character first appeared in Whiz

Comics #2 (February 1940). With a premise that taps into adolescent fantasy, Captain Marvel is the alter-ego of Billy Batson, a youth working as a radio news reporter who has been chosen to be a champion of good by the "magicians in fantasy" wizard Shazam. Whenever Billy speaks the wizard's name, he is instantly struck by a magic lightning bolt that transforms him into an adult superhero empowered with the abilities of six legendary figures. I loved him so much that I often ran through the house with a towel around my neck yelling out "Shazam." I quickly found out that the word only worked for Billy on TV.

Since I have been through some storms of my own (Hurricanes Alicia, Allison, Rita and now that bad brother named Ike), I have found a new magic word. Like Peter, I have found empowerment in the name of the Lord Jesus. Do you know the magic word? Or should I say, do you know the true identity of Jesus? It took two storms for the disciples to understand it, but thank God they did. I dare you to call that name when life's challenges face you. ᴄ☙ᴐ

Healing in Unfavorable Situations
(Mark 3:1-6)

◦⟨C❀Ↄ⟩◦

REV. DR. DAVID K. BRAWLEY

St. Paul Community Baptist Church
Brooklyn, New York

April 4, 2008 marked the 40th anniversary of the assassination of the Rev. Dr. Martin Luther King Jr. Recently, new light and analysis have been shed upon some of the most controversial speeches of Dr. King. One such speech made from the pulpit of the historic Riverside Church in 1967 was entitled "Beyond Vietnam: A Time to Break Silence," when Dr. King vehemently opposed the war in Vietnam. His fiery prophetic utterances exposed the shame of the nation. In this message Dr. King said, "A time comes when silence is betrayal," and he identified America as the greatest purveyor of violence in the world today. Many historians believe that this politically provocative speech ensured the assassination of this prophet of non-violence. (It appears that there is never a convenient time for the truth.)

Revealed and exposed truth can also seem untimely and inappropriate to others trapped by paralyzing fear. On April 16, 1963, a letter was directed to clergy who opposed the actions of Dr. King. His critics had questioned what they called the *unwise and untimely acts* of civil disobedience rendered on behalf of the racially oppressed residents of Birmingham, Alabama. In this historic letter, known as "The Letter from the Birmingham Jail," Dr. King, from this prison cell, questioned what he believed to be misplaced concern by his fellow clergymen. Dr. King said, "You deplore the demonstrations taking place in Birmingham. But your statement, I am sorry to say, fails to express a similar concern for the conditions that brought about the demonstrations." In Dr. King's eloquent and passionate refutation of his colleagues' viewpoint, he stressed that there was a divine pressure placed upon servants of the Lord to spread His message and work of justice, even if the timing appeared to be unfavorable and sometimes personally threatening.

CHRIST HEALS EVEN WITHOUT PERMISSION OF MEN

Similarly, this text found in the third chapter of Mark's Gospel is not so much about a man with a withered hand, although his obedience and faith were crucial to his healing. It is really about a Christ of controversy who demands obedience and supplies needs in spite of unfavorable situations.

What do I mean by "unfavorable"? Perhaps I should define the word "favorable" first. Favorable suggests pleasant, perfect conditions in which men are in charge of the process and have measurable input concerning the final outcome. What is so wonderful about our text is that Jesus does not require favorable conditions to be in place in order for Him to heal. The good news is that Jesus does not need predictions, platitudes, power or the permission of men to heal, deliver or set free.

One of my good friends and a co-laborer in the Gospel shared with me one day in a personally revealing moment the anguish that one goes through when plagued with a chronic medical condition. He divulged that his greatest disappointment came while being tested for an operation that would have healed him of his affliction. However, the conditions were not perfect; the results of the medical tests showed that this was not the right time for his surgery. Walking me through his ordeal, I could feel the anticipation of *what he thought* it was going to be like to be healed. Phone calls were placed, and excitement was in the air; but the conditions were not favorable. By the way, this was not a pity party but a display of faith, similar to Job when he said, "Though he slay me, yet will I trust him" (Job 13:15). But I could not help but hang on to every word when my friend said, "Do you know how perfect everything has to be in order for a surgeon to perform a surgery?"

I am glad to report that you can still shout when every detail does not match up with your desired outcome, because God is still God. As a matter of fact, in the face of our greatest opposition God can still bring us through. He can still bring a clean thing out of an unclean thing. He is still able to do exceedingly abundantly above all that we ask or think (Eph. 3:20), even when earthly circumstances are not perfectly aligned.

The first verse says that Jesus has again entered the synagogue, the place of instruction and worship, but this time it is the scene of controversy. The irony is that in the place dedicated to maintaining the spiritual well-being of the adherents of Judaism, a healing from Jesus is considered controversial.

One wonders what they have been praying for. Could it be that because they were not the sole conduits of God's power, this hardness of heart has caused them to shun and slander the answer to another man's prayers? If Jesus heals this man, He will be accused of performing a work on the Sabbath day, a violation punishable by death according to the Law of Moses. Religious leaders have been tracking the activities of Jesus since He healed a man with an unclean spirit in their synagogue; for they questioned among themselves, saying, "What is this? What new doctrine is this? For with authority He commands even the unclean spirits, and they obey Him" (Mark 1:27).

LIFE-ALTERING OR LIFE-THREATENING?

Knowing that it was not unusual for Jesus to heal, they plotted against Him, hoping that compassion would cause Him to heal this man. Now the Law made provisions for healing on the Sabbath as long as the injury or affliction was considered life threatening. This situation, while not life threatening, by any estimation was life altering. Jesus risked possible execution for a situation that was not of dire importance but would provide unimaginable positive change.

God is not only concerned about situations in our lives that are life threatening but also those that are life altering. For years I have been impressed and impacted by the compassion of Jesus toward overwhelming life situations, such as the resurrections of Lazarus, the Nain widow's only son and Jairus' daughter. Those were life-threatening situations. Now we can rejoice because Jesus is willing to address life-altering situations. What is a life-altering situation? It's a situation that did not take your life but changed it in such an adverse way you almost wish it had. It's a situation you're forced to live with but wish you could change. It's not all over; it just feels that way. In this moment Jesus reveals His compassion and demonstrates that He is concerned about that which concerns you and me.

Was this man's condition so severe that Jesus could not wait for the next day to heal him? I guess that depends upon who you talk to. If you converse with the Pharisees, they would obviously tell you that this man's condition should be addressed on a day other than the Sabbath. However, it was not their hand that was withered. Did they understand what it must have been like for this man to have a withered hand? Luke tells us that it was his right hand, which is synonymous with power, work and writing.

What is worse is that this man has a hand, but it is withered. Therefore, he has to be reminded daily of a hand that cannot function properly. Perhaps this atrophied hand belongs to a craftsman who once earned his living by his hands. Maybe he used to play some ancient game of basketball with his son. It is probable that this very hand used to caress the smooth skin of his wife. He was unable to function normally in society.

I suppose if we had asked this man if he could wait another day, he might have pointed to the fact that Jesus was present and willing to heal. Remember, the man did not ask to be healed. Jesus told him to stand forward in the middle of the room and receive his healing. I'm sure this man knew what day of the week it was, but I don't think he really cared about all that right then because a healing was about to take place.

While it is important to know something about this man's condition, it is equally important to diagnose the waiting and watching crowd. Why would they seek to bring charges against the Master? The same Jesus who healed people throughout the region of Galilee had also taught in their synagogues and transformed many lives. (The word *watch* in the text means more than an inquisitive glance, but a view toward bringing an accusation against Him.) In other words, they were ready to arrest Jesus, offer this healing as evidence and subpoena the man with the withered hand. They wanted Jesus to incriminate Himself, thus ending His public ministry and continuing their attempt to control and oppress others by their twisted interpretation of the Law.

Let me park parenthetically and pose this query. If the man did not request the healing, why did Jesus offer it? I suggest that Jesus could be seen as the provoker in this instance. He knew what His adversaries' plans were, yet according to the Law He still engaged in questionable activity. I believe that Jesus was ready to give them something to talk about. These lifeless Pharisees were trying to slander Jesus and sway public opinion against Him. The actions of Jesus remind us that we cannot wait for the favor of crowds to do what is in line with the call of God upon our lives. We don't need permission from others, but sometimes we have to give ourselves permission to be what God has created us to be.

OBEYING GOD IN AWKWARD SITUATIONS

Let us now turn our attention to the response of Jesus to His enemies. After calling the man with the withered hand forward, He raises the question in the fourth verse, "Is it lawful on the Sabbath day to do good or to do evil? To save life, or to kill?" But they keep silent. Jesus likens the healing of this man to doing good; not healing this man would be considered evil. Now, everyone present knows that the only way Jesus can justify healing this man is to prove that this is a life-or-death matter. However, Jesus presents a logical *opposite* perspective, showing them that the Sabbath is a matter of life and not death.

For the Sabbath was given to bring man into an intentional day of rest and renewal in the presence of God. Just because you take a day off doesn't necessarily mean that you observe the Sabbath. The Sabbath is really about renewal in the presence of God. The act of healing this man is therefore consistent with the divine intent for the Sabbath.

Jesus can make some demands upon our lives at the most awkward times, such as "Love your enemies and do good to those who despitefully use you" (Matt. 5:44) and "If a man smites you on your right cheek, offer to him the other" (Matt. 5:39). Being disciples of Jesus often puts us in the position to have to obey Him in some awkward situations.

This is the case of the man with the withered hand. He is told to stand forward. Synagogues were designed so that adherents to Judaism would sit around the walls and listen as the Scriptures were read and lessons were presented. In this instance, Jesus tells the man with the withered hand to step in view of everyone present. This is not a suggestion but a command, which means that this man is now on display for the Lord.

This is an interesting point. The commands of Jesus not only put me on the spot, but my obedience to Christ also puts Him on the spot. There may be times when trials and tribulations have made you feel like a mere shell and symbol of what you once were. Why is that? Perhaps you have not stepped forward. Note this direction. Although your situation has not changed, you are challenged to step forward. Don't be afraid to listen to Jesus when He says in the midst of your enemies to step forward.

If this wasn't enough, Jesus says, "Stretch out your hand"—the same hand that has been withered, possibly due to an accident or disease. Jesus says to put it out there. The man whose hand seemed to have no life left in it was told by Jesus to put it out there. In other words, "Go further." I am certain that this man is familiar with what happened to the leper in the first chapter of Mark. This man did not have to stretch out his hand to be healed. As a matter of fact, Jesus did the unthinkable for him; He touched him. He could have employed the same method for the man with the withered hand, so why did He make him stretch out his hand?

There is a sense in which Jesus healed the man, but He Himself did no work. The man did the work, but Jesus provided the miracle. Likewise, if you do the work, Jesus will provide the miracle. If you provide the prayer, Jesus will provide the answer. If you provide the faith, Jesus will provide the way out. If you provide the seed, Jesus will provide the harvest. If you provide the obedience, He will provide the blessing:

- Abraham provided the altar; God supplied the sacrifice.
- David provided the slingshot; God supplied the victory.
- Peter provided the net; Jesus supplied the fish.
- Moses provided a rod; God supplied a divided Red Sea.
- Noah provided the ark; God supplied the rainbow.
- Rahab the harlot provided lodging; God gave Israel the city.

According to the Law, the man with leprosy could not be touched, so Jesus touched him. The man with the withered hand could not reach, so Jesus told him to stretch out what he had. The record states that the man stretched forth his hand, and it was restored as whole as the other. By his compliance, he experienced life the way it was supposed to be. Similarly, when we obey the commands of Jesus—even if the conditions and situation seem to be unfavorable—He can restore life back to the way it should be. Hallelujah! ༺☙⌘❧༻

Holding On to Your Dreams
(Joshua 14:6-7a, 10b-11)

⁌ ⊂❀⊃ ⁍

REV. DR. LESLIE D. BRAXTON

New Beginnings Christian Fellowship
Renton, Washington

In his signature composition, "Montage of a Dream Deferred," poet laureate Langston Hughes inquires,

> What happens to a dream deferred?
> Does it dry up like a raisin in the sun?
> Or fester like a sore and then run?
> Does it stink like rotten meat?
> Or crust and sugar over like a syrupy sweet?
> Maybe it just sags like a heavy load
> Or does it explode?
> Dream within a dream,
> Our dream deferred

Our Judeo-Christian Western culture romanticizes dreaming. Many of the iconic biblical personalities are quickly remembered for their dreams. The legacy of Jacob, the colorful, complex patriarch and progenitor of Israel's twelve tribes, is inseparable from his dream of a ladder stretching from heaven down to earth with celestial beings trafficking back and forth.

There was Joseph, the 11th of Jacob's 12 sons, who spoke to his brothers and father of his dream of a future time when the world would bow in obeisance to him, *including them!*

At the heart of our American idealism lies the "American dream." It is the notion that in this nation any citizen—regardless of race, class, gender, religion or nation of origin—can rise from rags to riches through hard work and a little good fortune.

African-Americans place a high premium on the enterprise of dreaming. Martin Luther King Jr. stood on the steps of the Lincoln

Memorial and told America, *"I have a dream."* The impact of what Dr. King spoke has since demonstrated the power of a clearly and compellingly articulated dream to pull an entire nation out of a dark and sinful past and into a brighter and better future.

Not surprisingly then, we have become a nation of dreamers. High school students dream of going off to college and living free from Mom and Dad's restrictions. College kids dream of graduation, then a quick ascent up the corporate ladder and endless acquisition of all the adult toys and status symbols that they can grab along the way.

Parents also dream. They too dream of their children going off to college, the military, or wherever they can get them to go—just to get them off their hands so that they can drive their own cars again and spend their own money on themselves again.

Every year thousands of wannabe superstars compete to become the next American Idol, while tens of millions of closet-wannabes vicariously chase stardom simply by joining the addicted audience of anonymous viewers—*dreaming!*

The poet Paul Laurence Dunbar lets us know that even the homeless have dreams, if only of "a crust of bread and a corner to sleep in."

WHAT HAPPENS TO A DREAM DEFERRED?

In "Montage of a Dream Deferred," Langston Hughes sobers the euphoria of dreaming when he asks, "What happens to a dream deferred?" What happens to the dreamer when there appears to be no practical means of realizing the noble aim? What happens to the dreamer when his or her mental flight gets stuck in an unending circumstantial holding pattern? What happens to the visionary when his or her God-inspired motion is brought to the floor of the body of Christ, only to be tabled indefinitely or rejected outright by a pack of dream-killing wolves wearing sheep's clothing?

That is the question that shimmers from our text when we read the story of Caleb, the courageous Jephunite. For 40 years Caleb's dream had been deferred, not because of any unreadiness or unwillingness on his part, but rather due to the unbelief and wicked deeds of others to whom his dream was inextricably tied.

Caleb was among the 12 spies whom Moses dispatched from Israel's camp at Kadesh-Barnea to go over into Canaan and bring back a report on what was waiting on the other side of the Jordan River. Moses, their leader, needed tactical information that would help him shape his strategy for invading and subduing a land that was already occupied by many different people, none of whom had any plans of leaving.

When the spies returned to Israel's camp, they provided Moses with both a majority report and a minority report. Ironically, both reports agreed that the land indeed was flowing with milk and honey. Both reports presented evidence of the fertile valleys and sun-drenched hillsides, from which they had snatched bundles of fat grapes and sweet figs. In fact, both reports presented identical profiles on the land and the people who occupied it. The facts were not at all in dispute.

Nonetheless, there was a dispute, not over the facts *per se*, but over the divergent conclusions that the presenters of the respective reports drew from the facts. The majority report concluded that Israel should abort any current or future plans for entering Canaan—and even *return to Egypt!* Why? They had seen great cities behind fortressed walls that looked impenetrable. They had seen the mighty sons of Anak, whose numbers could not be numbered and who towered over them like giants and made them feel like grasshoppers by comparison. Also, they had seen the hosts of Amalekites encamped in the south, along with the armies of Amorites, Jebusites and Hittites encamped in the mountains and the hosts of Canaanites encamped by the sea and the shores of the Jordan. When they added it all up, they had seen enough to convince them: "We would not be able to go up against them because they are stronger than we are!" (Num. 13:31). To the contrary, Caleb and Joshua presented a minority report that offered a distinctly different conclusion: "Let us go up at once, and possess it; for we are well able to overcome it."

How could this be? Were Joshua and Caleb naïve? Were they reckless zealots who cared nothing for the facts? Were they simple-minded ideologues who went beyond the reach of reason and were now ready to plunge their entire nation into war with their eyes wide shut?!

Hardly! Joshua and Caleb's confident and unwavering resolve flowed out of two attributes of God that they never lost sight of. First, God doesn't lie. Second, God cannot fail. The God of Abraham had sworn to give them a land that was flowing with milk and honey. If God said it, He surely could bring it to pass. The Red Sea crossing had answered any questions in their mind about God's capacity in the midst of crisis. The supply of manna and quail in the wilderness had resolved any questions they could ever have had about God's ability to provide. For Joshua and Caleb, despite what they had *seen*, the call was an easy one: "We are well able to overcome it!" The question for Joshua and

Caleb was not, "How can victory be possible in the face of such odds?" Rather, the true question of faith before Israel was, "How can we doubt God after all that He has already done?!"

A story is told of an elderly, uneducated black woman who was a custodial worker in an inner-city high school for at-risk students. A shutdown of the city's subway system caused several of the teachers to be unable to get to work on one particular morning. This forced the principal to instruct the old cleaning woman to put down her mop and bucket and supervise one of the classrooms until he could get more teachers to the school.

The old woman knew that her task was simply to keep a classroom of difficult students from destructively exploiting an unexpected staffing crisis. So she decided to work from her strengths. She talked with the students about faith, telling them, "If the Lord told me to get up and walk through that door over there, I would get up right now and go do it." An outburst of laughter suddenly came from the class, followed by a mocking statement from a class spokesman: "Lady, I know you're old and obviously you can't see very well because there is no door over there where you're pointing." Without hesitation, the old woman shot back, "That's what I'm trying to teach you, child. You see, if the Lord told me to walk through a door over there, I would get up and start walking that way because I know that by the time I got over there, He would have made a door!"

Moses, the leader, dismissed all negative prognostications and began to make preparations to move into the land. And that's when the "stuff" got started.

The presenters of the majority report chose to circumvent the authority of Moses and took their case directly to the people. They moved insidiously throughout the camp with the efficiency of an airborne virus, spreading doubt and fear like contagions. In short order, the people who had been on a march toward destiny and greatness took up stones to execute Moses and were ready to elect a captain to take them *back to Egypt!*

But, at the very peak of their panic, God showed up in His glory! And when He showed up, He also spoke up: "How long will this people provoke ME? How long will it be before they believe ME, when I have already shown them such signs and wonders? I'm going to put the fulfillment of the promise 'on hold' while I smite them with pestilence and purge this nation of this stubborn element."

For 40 years the lights went out! For 40 years Israel wandered away from her true greatness and staggered in aimless patterns of repetitious confusion. And for 40 years Caleb's dream of an inheritance in the land of promise was deferred, left drying on the vine like "a raisin in the sun."

Can you imagine how Caleb (and Joshua) must've felt having their dream deferred by the foolishness of others? Perhaps it's like living in a nation that promises "life, liberty and the pursuit of happiness," yet an individual from *your* race is counted as 3/5 of a human being and treated more like a thing to be played with than a person to be reckoned with. Perhaps it's like being promised 40 acres and a mule, but instead you get slavery repackaged as sharecropping, Jim Crow and the homegrown terrorism of the Ku Klux Klan. Perhaps it's like being promised a "war on poverty," but instead your son gets sent to fight an immoral and illegal war in the jungles of Southeast Asia against another historically oppressed people of color. Perhaps it's like being promised a "war on drugs," but instead you get an undeclared war on *your community* via a criminally unjust criminal justice system that has one form of justice for the white and wealthy and a caricature of justice for the black, brown and poor. Perhaps it's like hearing an optimistic Martin Luther King Jr. say in 1963, "I have a dream," but just one year later hearing the same Martin Luther King say, "They've turned my dream into a nightmare."

EXPLODE, ROT...OR WAIT ON GOD!

Langston Hughes suggests in his signature poem that there are only two things that can happen to a "dream deferred." It can either "explode" or "rot."

In the 1960s, frustration exploded in poor urban ghettos, where black masses turned to rioting and burning their own communities. Martin Luther King Jr. commented at the time that "rioting is the language of the unheard."

It can be argued that the rise and prominence of Fatah, Hamas and Hezbollah are essentially the organized political explosions of a displaced and frustrated Palestinian people who are legitimately discontented with both the unrelenting Israeli occupation of Palestinian territories and the uneven-handed mediation of Western empires who call themselves brokers of peace in the Middle East.

But while some people explode in the face of deferment, others simply succumb to some form of stinking rot. Every single night, lost and restless young men idly stroll the streets of our cities with their hands shoved deep in their pockets, pushing the doors of life open with limp shoulders. Rotting!

As America's social safety net continues to erode, the homeless population continues to swell and diversify. The deinstitutionalized mentally ill are joined by poor (and often battered) women and children, teenage runaways, physically and mentally maimed veterans of the armed forces, the chemically addicted and people who were living from paycheck to paycheck until they finally missed a paycheck. Perhaps the greatest sign of our society's growing apathy may be our strange comfort we derive from bulging internal colonies of rotting souls!

Even in the church you see this ugly, insidious rotting. While some of God's children are "growing in grace and the knowledge of our Lord and Savior," others merely go through the motions of religion. They attend worship each week by force of habit; but they apparently take nothing in, and they certainly give nothing out. They just sit there, week after week, feeding addictively on a steady diet of sickening familiarity. They display no joy in their walk with God. They offer no testimony of God's goodness and mercy at work in their lives. They provide no ministry service that strengthens the body of Christ or relieves the suffering of others. They just sit in *their* seats and rot!

Well, amazingly, after 45 years of waiting, Caleb has neither rotted nor exploded. He declares that he is just as strong now as he was a generation earlier. The gleam is still in his eyes, and the fire still burns in his belly. Caleb has defied the cynical prognostications of the poet Hughes. He knew that frustrated dreamers are not limited to a choice between rotting and exploding. There's a third, more creative choice that's available to the mind of faith. You can WAIT ON THE LORD!

The phrase "wait on the Lord" may seem to be overused and trivial. But place it in the context of Caleb's spiritual odyssey, and you can see what it's really all about. For 45 years, Caleb waited *in* faith for the fulfillment of the dream that he had taken *on* faith. He trusted God for both the substance and the timing of the dream. Often in our spiritual journeys, we backpedal from our destiny because things don't happen soon enough. We confuse deferment with default, failing to realize that time is an ingredient and not the enemy to our dreams.

In Saint Peter's Basilica in Rome, there is a cast bronze statue of the patron saint Peter, the vicar of Jesus Christ, in the nave of the church. Although scholars are unsure of the sculptor—some suggest it was Arnolfo di Cambio (1245-1308), who began building the Duomo in Florence—tradition claims that this statue is the product of the early church. Consequently, this depiction of Peter is particularly venerated by the faithful. Through the centuries, pilgrims to Rome have touched Peter's extended right foot out of homage to him. Now it is noticeably smooth and concave, compared to the rest of the statue.

Again and again, the Bible points out the fact that God smoothes out rough situations, in part, with the touch of time. God spent 45 years in the wilderness smoothing out the hearts and minds of a people who had proven at Kadesh-Barnea to be too stubborn and too weak of faith to walk in His promises. And while God was smoothing things out throughout the nation, Caleb had to wait.

Caleb's life tells the story of people with dreams who have to learn to wait on God, knowing and trusting that He's up to something creative, even when it seems like nothing is happening. Parents with prodigal children have to learn to pray, enforce discipline, encourage, role model and *wait*. Spouses in a marital impasse have to pray, forgive, dialogue and *wait*. Oppressed people have to pray, organize, struggle and *wait*. Pastors with a vision for their congregation and its ministry have to pray, work, lead, love and *wait!* The touch of time is necessary for the delivery of our dreams. God needs time to smooth things out!

Having waited for 45 years, Caleb did more than just preserve his claim to an inheritance. Perhaps even more significant was his experience of the "keeping power of God." At 85 years of age, Caleb was still physically strong, mentally sharp, emotionally intact and spiritually whole because God "kept" him during those long, tedious years of waiting. While all of his peers, excluding only Joshua, were consumed by a wilderness of hardships, Caleb only grew wiser and stronger.

Perhaps the central lesson to be learned from the life of Caleb is that it matters not so much that you wait—as much as it matters *how* you wait. If he had waited grudgingly or resentfully, surely the seeds of bitterness would have grown a harvest of rage or resignation in his spirit. If he had waited restlessly or nervously, almost certainly the internal anxiety would have psychosomatically eaten away at his health. If in waiting he had become covetous of the perceived gains of others, he surely would have driven away friends and burned personal and strategic bridges with the flames of petty jealousy.

But because Caleb waited in faith, the very toll of time itself had been diminished: "I am still as strong today as the day Moses sent me out." The expected ravages of time had been postponed. Caleb is not just "alive"; he remains "full of life." Waiting in faith has blessed him with both longevity and vitality. Yes, he has lived to see the day when God has smoothed out all the barriers to the fulfillment of his dream. But perhaps as equally important, he still has the strength to seize the moment with the capacity to engage in new battles that will surely come with new opportunity. Forty-five years later, Caleb is still up for the fight. God has kept him!

In the life of Caleb, God proved that He's not just a keeper of dreams. He is also a keeper of dreamers.

Early in the 19th century, a young man in London aspired to become an author. Although he was obsessed with writing, his life was hard. His father spent time in jail because of his inability to pay his debts. The young man finished only four years of schooling. He worked at menial jobs and slept in a dreary, rat-infested attic while pursuing his dream. Story after story was rejected. At one point the aspirant became so discouraged and embarrassed, he would sneak out at night to mail his manuscripts.

Finally the day arrived when one of his pieces was accepted. Although he was not paid for the story, his confidence soared: An editor had recognized his talent! From this unlikely background emerged Charles Dickens, because God is both a keeper of dreams *and* dreamers.

The songwriter, F.I. Eiland, wrote,

> In my weakness be my strength
> In my trials all
> Be Thou near me all the day,
> Hear my every call
>
> Keep my heart, and keep my hand,
> Keep my soul, I pray!
> Keep my tongue to speak Thy praise,
> Keep me all the way!

One Life to Live
(Psalm 42:1)

⋄

REV. FRANCE B. BROWN JR.

College of Biblical Studies
Houston, Texas

One of the great success stories of the Looney Tunes cartoon series launched by Warner Bros. was the pairing of Tweety Bird and Sylvester the cat. Tweety was the good-natured, yellow-feathered, blue-eyed domestic canary who happily matriculated through life accompanying his darling owner Granny. Sylvester was the black-and-white tuxedo cat with a slobbering, squeaky lisp that showed much pride in himself and persistence in his quest to capture and eat Tweety.

Most of their shows featured a standard format. Granny carried Tweety in his cage as she went about her regular routine of shopping at the market, visiting the library or doing her good deed for the day. In a nearby alley, Sylvester rummaged through heaps of open trash, garbage cans or dumpsters meticulously scavenging for food. Suddenly he spots the unsuspecting pair and inconspicuously makes his way toward them, hiding behind anyone and anything that might give him momentary and necessary cover as he stalks what he believes to be an easy victim. Somehow, just before he is ready to pounce on his inno-cent prey, Tweety has a sneaky suspicion—a sixth-sense revelation. It is then that he looks into the camera and gives us his signature line, "Uh-oh, I tawt I taw a puddy tat." He takes a look in Sylvester's direc-tion and then confirms his suspicion by declaring, "I did, I did taw a puddy tat!" For the rest of the episode, Sylvester progressively employs more diabolical and elaborate schemes and devices, trying to capture his meal. Unfortunately for him, all of his tricks fail miserably, usual-ly due to their inherent flaws.

There was, however, one episode that deviated from the normal for-mat of the Tweety-Sylvester saga. This episode begins with the chase already in progress. Sylvester chases Tweety up buildings, down buildings, across the street, in and out of alleys, around corners, over fences and through neighborhoods and houses. All of a sudden, Sylvester gets hit by a car. He dies and goes to hell. There in Satan's court, the Devil tells him, "Sylvester, you're a cat with nine lives. Now you have eight left. Go out and get Tweety!" He goes back to earth and chases Tweety and gets hit by a bus. He dies and goes to hell. There in Satan's court, the Devil tells him, "Sylvester, you're a cat and you have seven lives left. Go out and get Tweety!" He goes back to get Tweety and dies and dies and dies again. So he goes back before Satan in his court. Satan says to him, "Sylvester, you're a cat. You had nine lives. Now you only have one left. But I've got faith in you. Go back and pursue Tweety." Sylvester ponders the exhortation of Satan. He looks to his right and sees, standing beside a wall in this deep, dark, dreary dungeon, those eight lives that he lost in his pursuit of the elusive Tweety. They were flattened, battered, mangled, shredded and scorched—the evidence of his hard times. After careful consideration of Satan's words and the reality of his own experiences, he turns and runs away screaming, "No! No! No! I give up! I give up! I give up!" Thus, he saved his last and final life. Good for ol' Sylvester.

Unfortunately, beloved, you and I are not like Sylvester. We don't have nine lives. We don't have multiple lives to expend. We don't have the convenience of countless lives to sacrifice. We don't have the luxury of disposable days. We only have one life to live. The questions that each of us must answer are these: "What does God want me to do with this one life?" "What does God expect of me?" To find out, I invite you to turn your attention to the 42nd Psalm. Verse one reads, "As the deer pants for the water brooks, so my soul pants for Thee, O God" (NASB).

Psalm 42 is known as a Lament Psalm. Here, the psalmist cried out to God because of a disturbing situation that he could not ignore. He was faced with some agonizing circumstance that he could not avoid—a perplexing plight that he could not change. He was met with an insufferable condition from which he could not escape. This psalm was written by King David while he was fleeing for his life from his son Absalom. With a fresh reading of the first verse, it seems that David was on his way to church, caught up in the bliss of divine worship and the majesty of God's presence. It seems like he woke up this morning with his mind stayed on Jesus. But this just wasn't the case. He was, in fact, running from Jerusalem, lamenting the consequences of his own sin.

In 2 Samuel 11, the setting was springtime, the season when kings led their armies into battle. David abdicated his responsibility to Joab and stayed home in Jerusalem. Later that night, David decided to take a little walk on the rooftop of the king's house. Now, he wasn't just putting one foot in front of the other. The Hebrew grammar gives us a far more significant picture of David's movement. In Hebrew, how a word is written tells us how the word looks in action. The Hebrew term for "walk" is *halak*. It means to "proceed" or "move about." It is used here in a form called the hithpael stem. Used this way, *halak* means to "walk about as an expression of dominion." It is an exercise of authority. In other words, David casually yet pridefully strolled on his rooftop taking stock of "his" kingdom. (Take care, beloved; pride goes before a fall.) Suddenly, something happened that stopped David in his tracks. He saw something. It was a woman, not just any woman, but an exceedingly beautiful woman. To make matters worse, she was naked and bathing. David learned that she was Bathsheba, the wife of Uriah and the daughter of Eliam. He sent for her and initiated a sexual relationship with her. David's sin of slothfulness metastasized into lust, then adultery, then murder and finally into deception and corruption. For nearly a year, he almost got away with it, just like you and I almost get away with our messes.

Later, the prophet Nathan confronted David with a story of a treacherous man. David's condemning judgment of fourfold restitution against this man came back to haunt him in the worst way. The child whom he conceived with Bathsheba died—that's one. His son Amnon raped his daughter Tamar—that's two. His son Absalom killed Amnon for raping his daughter Tamar—that's three. Now Absalom, who killed Amnon for raping his daughter Tamar, turned the people's hearts against him and was hunting him like an animal to kill him—that's four. Now, I know what David must have been thinking. As he fled Jerusalem like a defeated loser, he had to be screaming to himself, "I don't believe this. All of these problems in my life for 15 minutes of pleasure!" But in the calamity of his sin and the doldrums of despair, he had the good sense to look toward heaven and pray, "As the deer pants for the water brooks, so my soul pants for Thee, O God." By David's plea, we get an idea of what God wants us to do with our one life to live.

BE CONFIDENT IN GOD!

The first thing that God wants you to do with your one life is to **be confident in Him.** David said, "As the deer *pants* for the water brooks, so my soul *pants for* Thee, O God." To express his confidence in God,

David draws an explicit comparison of the pursuit of water by a deer with his pursuit of God. The Hebrew term for "pants" is *arag*. It means as the deer craves water, as the deer desires water, as the deer needs water, as the deer is drawn to water, as the deer thirsts for and yearns for water. The deer craves water because water is what it needs to sustain life. David pursues God because life has convinced him now more than ever that he has no greater need than God. He needs God, more than his temporal desires, more than his accomplishments and achievements. I am told that a human being can live 40 days without food, but he can live only three days without water. Water is the universal source of life. You can't survive without it. David is trying to help us understand that, just as the deer understands that it needs water more than anything else, we should be persuaded that more than anything else we need God.

Through David's actions, God says to you and me, "I want you to pursue Me." God is saying, "I want you to want Me like I want you. I want you to desire Me more than your money. Crave Me more than your job. Respect Me more than your boss. Strive for Me more than for promotions. Yearn for Me more than your 401k, your car, your house, your husband, your wife, your children, your church, your habits or your parking spot—more than fame or fortune or favor with others. I want you to want Me like I want you."

David's confidence in God is demonstrated by his pursuit of Him. The fact that he craves Him, yearns for Him, desires Him and thirsts after Him lets us know that he places his hope squarely in the providential capability of God. He depends on Him. He rests in His hands. He says, "As the deer pants for the water brooks, so my soul pants *for* Thee,

O God." The King James Version translates "for" as "after." This word comes from the Hebrew term *elekah*, a preposition that expresses movement of thoughts, emotions and will in the direction of someone or something. It literally means "toward." David holistically moves his life Godward. He is thinking with God's mind. He is feeling with God's heart. He is acting according to God's will for the sake of God's glory. His emotions, his mind and his spirit moves in the direction of God. In Psalm 25:1, David says, "*Toward* thee, O Lord, I lift up my soul." His craving and yearning is geared *toward* the Almighty.

Let me see if I can help you get this. During my first year of seminary, a loved one was involved in a car accident. An attorney referred me to a particular doctor. During the visit with the doctor, he asked, "What do you want me to write down?" I'm thinking to myself, "Hey, I'm a preacher, not a physician." On the second visit, he said something that struck me as strange. He said, "We will simply split the money." "What money?" I replied. He said, "The personal injury protection money that comes from the insurance company for the accident." Now, that was music to a poor seminary student's ears. Enthusiastic but suspicious, I contacted a friend who worked in the insurance industry. He informed me that what the doctor was proposing was illegal. It was insurance fraud. During the next visit, I told the doctor that we would not be back and that he should bill the insurance company for the services rendered. I never shall forget what he said to me: "I know that you're a straight-up guy and all, but don't you at least want some of this money?" The translation was, "I know that you call yourself a Bible-totin', hand-clapping, foot-stomping, saved, sanctified, filled-with-the-

Holy-Ghost, seminary-going, I-love-the-Lord, He-heard-my-cry, wanna-be-real preacher, but surely you can't pass this up, can you?"

In a split second, I thought, "Boy, I sure don't want to be convicted by the Holy Spirit for this." Then I thought, "Boy, I sure don't want to be convicted by the State of Texas for this, either." In that split second, I thought, "Lord, what will this say to this doctor about my confidence in You? What will it say to him about You? Can't You take care of Your own? What will this say to my loved one about my faith in You? Lord, what will this say to You about my trust in You?" I'm reminded of something I read once about trusting God: "Trust in yourself and you are doomed to disappointment. Trust in your friends and they will die and leave you. Trust in God and you will never be confounded, in time or eternity."

BE CANDID WITH GOD!

Not only does God want you to be confident in Him, but He also wants you to **be candid with Him**. David says, "As the deer pants for the water brooks, so *my soul* pants for Thee, O God." To be candid with God is to make your life open to Him. It is a life marked by transparency and authenticity toward God. In other words, God wants you to be real with Him: No more counterfeit faithfulness. No more long-distance relationship with Him. No more arm's-length spirituality. No more "on again-off again" devotion to Him. God is ready for some heart-to-heart time with you.

The problem, beloved, is that it's not always easy. You see, it's hard to be real in an age of manufactured reality. It is hard to be real with God, or anybody else for that matter, when you can simply manufacture your own existence. Think about it. If you don't like the color of your eyes, you can buy contacts that change the color of your eyes. If you don't like the color of your hair, that's O.K.; you can buy spray that changes the color of your hair. Let's say you don't like the length of your hair; never fear, you can buy extensions. You may think it's too expensive, but don't worry about that. You can buy yourself some hair at the Everything's-A-Dollar store these days. Just wait, in a minute Wal-Mart will launch its own line of hair. Let's say you don't like the texture of your hair; never fear, you can go to Sally's Beauty Supply and purchase some chemicals that will change the texture of your hair. If you don't like your nose, hey, you can get a nose job and take care of that. If you're dissatisfied with your lips, don't fret; you can have a substance injected into your lips to fix that, too. Oh, that's not all, beloved. Say there are other parts of your body that don't quite stay in place like they used to. They may droop here or sag there; don't worry, you can go to the doctor and have these things surgically altered. Oh yes, we live in an age where people can literally manufacture their own existence.

But David warns us that it's time to get real. He said, "I've faked it for far too long and look where it's gotten me—beaten, battered and broken-hearted." Notice that he says, "My *soul* pants for you, God." Don't miss that. One of my preaching heroes used to say, "Don't read the Bible too fast or you might miss something." Here, David uses a literary device called a synecdoche to emphasize something very important about himself. Now, a synecdoche substitutes one word for another in order to make a point. With a synecdoche, one can identify a specific part of something to represent the whole. For instance, back in the 1980s, I remember wanting to get some wheels for my prom date. Now,

I assure you that I was not simply interested in having four circular frames to look at. No, I wanted "a car." As a mischievous child, it was not uncommon for me to hear my mother say that she was going to break my "neck." I believe she had more parts of my body in mind.

"Soul," *nephesh*, is the inner part of David's being. It is that immaterial part of him that serves as the moral compass of his thoughts, feelings and actions. It is the inner man—the seat of his mind, will and emotions. David says that his pursuit of God is not simply an external exercise. He says, "God, I pursue You from the inside out." This isn't a show. This is not about performing. This is not about doing, but it's about being.

Likewise, we need to tell God: "I'm not simply going to pursue You on Sunday morning when the lights are on, the music is flowing and the choir is singing. No, I'm not simply going to pursue Your will on Wednesday when the crowd is watching. I'm not just going to perform; I am going to be. I'm going to pursue You, God, Monday through Friday at the job where I'm tempted to participate in the political ungodliness for the sake of advancement. I'll pursue You, whether I get a promotion or a pink slip. I'm going to pursue You on the weekend and walk in victory over my struggles. I'll pursue You at home while dealing with my wayward children, my stubborn husband or my uncooperative wife. Play time is over! I want to be real with You."

Our lack of being real with God reminds me of an experience I had at a McDonald's some time back. A lady came through the door with a gang of small children. She gave them permission to play in the children's area. After her order was ready, she called to one of the kids, "Brian, you guys come and get it." There was no response. Again, she cried out, "Brian, you guys come and get it," and again, no response. Then she did that thing that parents do to let their children know that they mean business. She shouted, "Brian Andrew Thomas, you get down here right now!" This time, Brian responded, "We don't want to come and get it; we want to play!" People of God, herein lies the problem with many of us. Here is the creator of the universe; the sustainer of life; the giver of life, peace and hope saying, "Come and get it! You need some relief, come and get it. You need love, come and get it. You need forgiveness, come and get it. You need a second chance, come and get it. You need a friend, come and get it. Whatever you need, I got it, so come and get it!" The sad part of this story is many of us are like those obstinate children. We don't want to come and get it. We want to play!

BE COMMITTED TO GOD!

Not only does God want you to be confident in Him and candid with Him, but He also wants you to **be committed to Him.** The text says, "As the deer *pants* for the water brooks, so my soul *pants* for Thee, O God." Here, the grammar of David's prayer helps us connect with God's truth. We said that to "pant," *arag*, means to pursue God, to crave and to yearn for Him. Now, it wouldn't make much sense to do this just one time or one day out of the week. The form of *arag* that David uses is what we call the imperfect aspect, which in this context tells us that he not only pursues God now, but he will continue to pursue Him. In other words, he communicates a consistency or commitment to crave, yearn and thirst for God. A deer does not simply look for water one day out of the week. He engages in a constant quest for the source of life. Now, I'm a city boy who knows very little about hunting, but I've been told that a deer will face death to get to some water. What will you face? What are you willing to risk to get to God?

One of my all-time favorite TV shows was *"Dallas."* On one particular episode, J.R. and his brother Bobby were embroiled in one of their customary confrontations. J.R. had accused Bobby of a lukewarm commitment to Ewing Oil. Bobby protested and declared that he was just as committed as J.R. They went back and forth, and neither would give an inch. Then J.R. gave one of his famous zingers that shut the conversation down and sent us to a commercial break. He said, "Bobby, you're not committed; you're involved. Take the breakfast you're eating—your ham and eggs. The chicken that provided the eggs was involved. The pig that provided the ham was committed."

You see, beloved, commitment means sacrifice. Something has to die. If you're going to be committed to God, that something is you. You will have to die to your will, your ways, your agenda and your desires. You will have to die to yourself. As the beloved hymn says, "All to Thee, my blessed Savior, I surrender all."

I mentioned earlier that it was unfortunate for us that we were not like Sylvester. I must admit I was a bit jealous of him. It seemed as though he got a better deal. After all, he had nine lives. Then I got to thinking. Sylvester had nine lives because he needed nine lives. I don't need nine lives. All I need is one Savior, and that one Savior has given to me more than nine lives. That Savior has given me eternal life. That Savior has given me abundant life. That Savior has given me the blessed life. That Savior has given me the victorious life. And unlike

Sylvester, when I die, I won't have to worry about facing Satan in any court because I am persuaded by the words of Albert E. Brumley:

Some glad morning when this life is o'er,
I'll fly away
To a home on God's celestial shore
I'll fly away

I'll fly away, oh glory, I'll fly away
When I die, hallelujah by and by,
I'll fly away.

Triumphant Faith For Troubled Times
(John 14:1)

DR. STEPHEN D.C. CORTS

Center Grove Baptist Church
Clemmons, North Carolina

Oxford, in the United Kingdom, is an enchanting and beautiful place. Called "The English Athens," the ancient university town has been described as "that sweet city of dreaming spires." Indeed, the Romantic poet William Wordsworth renounced his *alma mater* of Cambridge for his love of Oxford and her singular splendor.

But Oxford's long history as the "citadel of truth and beauty" has a dark side as well. In the center of the city, there is a cross of iron and stones embedded in Oxford's famous Broad Street near Balliol College. The simple black-and-white cross is a reminder of a time of deep trouble in England's religious history. It marks the place where three men were burned at the stake for their faith. They are known as the "Oxford Martyrs."

In his *Book of Martyrs* (1563), John Foxe tells the story of the tragic events that took place from 1554 to 1556. The bloody Queen Mary Tudor ruled England, and for those committed to biblical Christianity, they were troubled times. Three bishops—Hugh Latimer, Nicolas Ridley and Thomas Cranmer—found themselves charged with heresy and placed on trial in the university church of St Mary's. Among the reasons for the trial were their commitment to the belief in the sole sufficiency of Christ's atoning death for salvation and their refusal to compromise with the Catholic traditions and beliefs of the Queen. Eventually, Latimer and Ridley were punished together, while Cranmer's trial and martyrdom came later.

According to Foxe, Ridley arrived at the place of execution first. When Latimer arrived, the two embraced, and Ridley called his friend to practice great faith in a terrible time. He said, "Be of good heart, brother, for God will either assuage the fury of the flame, or else strengthen us to abide it." They both knelt and prayed before listening to an exhortation from a preacher calling on them to recant before death.

After the sermon, one of the officials pleaded, "Mr. Ridley, if you will revoke your erroneous opinions, you shall not only have liberty so to do, but also your life." "Not otherwise?" said Ridley.

"If you will not do so," replied the official, "there is no remedy: you must suffer for your deserts."

"Well," concluded Ridley, "so long as the breath is in my body, I will never deny my Lord Christ and His known truth. God's will be done in me."

The blacksmith wrapped a chain of iron around the waists of Ridley and Latimer. When the wood about Ridley's feet was lit, Latimer said, "Be of good comfort, Mr. Ridley, and play the man! We shall this day light such a candle, by God's grace, in England, as I trust never shall be put out."

As the fire rose, Latimer cried out, "O Father of heaven, receive my soul!" and he died almost immediately. Ridley, however, hung on, with most of his lower body having burned before he passed away. Such faith! Such deep faith in deeply troubled times!

We live in troubled times of our own—although our troubles are distinctly different from those of Latimer and Ridley. Our nation is in a protracted war on two fronts. The U.S. financial system is facing what some have called "its gravest crisis in modern history." Unemployment and home foreclosure rates are rising. Some of our largest banks are failing. Prominent mortgage lenders are collapsing or going into conservatorship. We are witnessing some of the largest bankruptcies in U.S. history. Credit is tightening. The once mighty Wall Street is in a meltdown and now turns to Washington for help. Washington finds that answers for our crisis are few, and good scenarios for our future are fewer still as the economic turmoil is spreading. Reports of lawmakers wrangling in heated shouting matches do little to instill confidence about our nation's condition. No one really knows what to do . . . or what will happen in the end.

Fear and uncertainty are growing and spreading almost unchecked, like kudzu in the South. While these are, indeed, very troubling times, the fact of the matter is that trouble is not extraordinary. In fact, trouble is a regular part of life.

As far as I can tell, there are three kinds of trouble: First, there is the trouble we make for ourselves. Second, there is the trouble others make for us. And, finally, there is the trouble that comes simply from living in a broken world. However it comes, trouble is a regular part of life.

The Bible affirms repeatedly that trouble is a fact of life that no one can escape:

- The Old Testament says, "Man's days are few and full of trouble" (Job 14:1).
- To His followers Jesus said plainly, "In this world you will have trouble" (John 16:33).

But the Bible shows us that *every trouble we face in life comes with an invitation to triumph over it by trusting God in Christ.* There is help and encouragement today for those who will take that invitation and make God's triumph a reality in their lives—regardless of the troubles we face as a nation or as individuals.

We come today to one of the darkest moments in the lives of Jesus' first followers. It is found in a beloved, classic text of John 14:1-6. From them we learn the first great secret to triumphing over trouble.

In the previous chapter, Jesus has gathered His disciples in an upper room for what is to be their last supper together. In essence, He says to them, "I have an announcement. I am going to be betrayed by one of you. What's more, I'm leaving you, and where I am going you cannot come."

This announcement shocks and astounds them and throws them into a panic. These are men who, except for one, have given their hearts and souls to Jesus. They have given up everything to follow Him: occupations, family, and their way of life. They love Him deeply and well because He has loved them so deeply and so well. Now He says to them words they do not want to hear and cannot fathom: "I am going to be leaving you. And where I am going you cannot come." So, they are devastated. Trouble has come.

In the 14th chapter, Jesus acts immediately to help them deal with this trouble that has come. He gives them direction and comfort—first in the form of a *command for trouble*, and then in the form of a *call to triumph*.

JESUS' COMMAND WHEN TROUBLE COMES

Jesus tells His disciples, "Do not let your heart be troubled." He addresses His disciples' concerns immediately by saying something to them that none of us would ever have expected. Right from the beginning, He makes it plain that the trouble they are feeling on the inside amidst this troubling news from the outside represents a *choice*.

Of course, many of us find it easier to give up and give in to troubled feelings on the inside when trouble comes on the outside. Indeed, most of us feel we have no choice, especially when the troubles we are facing are greater than we are and are more complicated than our minds can handle.

When these kinds of troubles come, we recognize how truly helpless we really are. In such times, we inevitably find that trouble moves in, takes over and will not go away. Perhaps we do not need the reminder, but the truth is that you and I never have life under control. With one phone call, a person's entire life can change forever.

In such times, it can seem that being troubled by trouble is the only possibility open to us. But Jesus shows us that *being troubled by trouble is not our only option*. Indeed, we might ask, "What other option do we have?" But look carefully, first of all, at **what** Jesus says: "Don't let your hearts be troubled . . ." The sense of this phrase is very strong, and it actually means: "*Stop* letting your heart be troubled." The idea here is that of stopping an action or activity that has already begun. And that activity is *trouble* on the inside that comes from the outside.

The word "trouble" here conveys the notion of a disturbance or an agitation. It is a picture for us of a heart that is without rest—a heart whose condition is like water roiling in a pot on a hot stove. And that is the place the disciples find themselves! On the basis of what they have heard, they find their hearts in motion—or better yet, in *commotion!*

But, look carefully with me at **how** Jesus says this. This is a *command* that has powerful implications. By commanding the disciples to stop, Jesus is implying that when trouble comes into their lives, they have both the *capacity* and the *choice* to decide to stop the trouble in their hearts. Their troubles do not have to triumph. Troubles do not have to confuse them with worry and paralyze them with fear.

I find this to be incredible news. I have never found worry to have a positive outcome. It has never helped me solve the first problem. In fact, it has almost always made things worse!

Positively, Jesus' command for handling trouble means that His disciples *can choose* to be untroubled in spite of it. Trouble on the outside must not necessarily mean anxiety, fear, confusion or defeat on the inside.

Negatively, Jesus' command for handling trouble means that whenever His disciples have a consistently agitated, disturbed heart over a matter, it is evidence of a personal choice to be troubled. It is proof of a choice to be in bondage on the inside to circumstances when Jesus has made a way for us to be truly free.

I would imagine there are many of us living with such troubled hearts—hearts distressed by finances, jobs, marriages, kids, school, the future or the past. And many believers are living in such defeat because trouble has come into their lives, and they have not been able to find a way to defeat it. The truth is that many of us are living with what seems to be a terminally troubled heart.

JESUS' CALL TO TRIUMPH

So Jesus says to you what He said to His disciples: "Stop!" And everything within us says in response, "Yes, Lord, but how?" Thankfully, Jesus helps us to know how with real success. Jesus adds to His command for trouble a call to triumph. He goes on to say, "Believe in God, believe also in Me." In this way, Jesus calls His disciples to triumph in their troubles by replacing the fear and worry that trouble brings with something called "faith."

Surely that sounds "churchy" and simple—too simple. Jesus' call to believers is simple, in a sense. His call in the midst of trouble is

"Believe!" Does it work? The answer of the Bible, from literally cover to cover, is, "Yes!" Indeed, in many ways the Bible is the story of faith triumphing over trouble, again and again! It demonstrates to us that God is always positively and powerfully at work on behalf of those who trust Him. This is the essential truth behind another classic text, Romans 8:28-29. Paul says, "And we know that God causes all things to work together for good to those who love God and are called according to His purpose [which is that they] become conformed to the image of His Son . . . ." God is always working all things together for our greatest good!

And so we can choose triumph by trusting—by replacing the fear that is natural with a faith that is supernatural! But just what is it that Jesus invites or calls us to do?

Jesus says, "You believe God, believe also in Me." The fuller meaning of this command is *Keep on believing* in God and *keep on believing* in Me." Jesus shows us that faith or trust in the midst of trouble is not simply a deliberate choice to stop worrying. It is also a deliberate choice to place our full confidence in the God we cannot see in spite of the trouble we do see.

Practically speaking, exercising faith in troubled times is an act whereby we relinquish doubt. Faith chooses to say, "Lord, I don't understand why this trouble has come. I don't understand what the answer is, but I relinquish the why and the how of it all to You."

This means that faith chooses *not* to say, "Lord, first You must explain to me the 'why's' for all of this and then I will trust You." It chooses not to say, "Father, You must also give me the 'how's' of Your solution to my trouble for me to consider and approve it before You do it." Instead, faith simply says, "Sovereign God, I am not going to ask why. I may not be able to understand Your answer! I am not going to ask You how. I do not dare decide for You what should be done to fix my problem. My prescription will do me more harm than good! Far better for me to rely on You as my heavenly Doctor to write the prescription I need for my problem. Far better for me to:

- **Wait** as You write it *and*
- **Wait** as You deliver it *and*
- **Wait** as You apply it to my life."

Faith in troubled times involves surrendering your self and your trouble even when you don't know His solution. But just *how* do we practice that kind of surrender?

Jesus suggests the first and fundamental step required whenever trouble appears. It is the first step that we must take if we're going to experience the triumph God says can be ours: **When trouble comes, we must first go and check the foundations of our faith in God.** We must go to the things of God upon which we have built our lives and see that they are still intact.

What are the foundations of true faith? The foundations of faith Jesus points to in the first verse essentially consist of the Person of God (**who** God is) and the work of God (**what** God has done, is doing and has promised to do).

In other words, Jesus invites us to keep on believing in who the Father is, what He has done, along with what He is now doing and has promised to do.

What power this prescription has! In changing, confusing, chaotic times, it is good and very necessary to remember that the Person, purposes and plans of God never change. He is the same yesterday, today and forever.

That means that:

> • If He genuinely *loved* you yesterday, you can be sure that He still loves you today.

> • If He *was faithful* to you yesterday, He will still be faithful to you today.

> • If He *had power* for your yesterday, He still has power for your today and your tomorrow.

He is *more than sufficient* for any trouble we face!

THREE TRUTHS FOR TROUBLED TIMES

Let me suggest **three pairs of questions and three great truths for troubled times** that believers can ask and rest in when trouble comes into their lives. They will help remind us of who the God is that we trust. They are vital questions and truths—questions and truths that you will need when your unexpected phone call comes:

1. What can God do and what can't He do?

The answer is that there is nothing that is impossible with Almighty God. The only thing that Scripture says God cannot do is to act contrary to His nature! For example, He cannot lie (Heb. 6:18).

A first great truth for trouble is this: **When trouble comes, there is nothing that can keep God from helping you. Our God is an omnipotent God. He has all the power there is.**

That is why it does not matter what your trouble is or how impossible it may seem to you: **There is no impossibility in the economy of**

God. In fact, it is the impossible things which come into our lives that allow us—if we walk through them with faith—to see the glory, the greatness and the goodness of our God! When trouble comes, it is important for us to remember and believe that God still has all the power to help us at the point of our need.

2. What does God know and what does He not know?

In Psalm 139, the psalmist says, "Where can I go from your presence? If I go to the heavens, you are there. If I go down to the depths, you are there. Such knowledge is too wonderful for me."

In the midst of trouble, God knows. God knows the trouble we are facing. He knows the pain we are feeling. What's more, He knows the answers we need! This means that you and I do not need to know the answers to our troubles . . . all we need to know is that **He knows the answer!**

A second great truth for trouble is this: *When trouble comes, God knows.* It is important for us to remember and believe that *no trouble we are experiencing has missed God's attention or taken Him by surprise. He knows the problem and its ultimate and best solution.*

3. Does God really love me and is there any trouble that can keep me from experiencing His love?

Sometimes in the midst of those troubles that come into our lives, we are tempted to want to know whether God cares. It doesn't take too many dark nights (and bright days that feel like dark nights) before we are tempted to say things like, "If God really loved me, how could He allow this to come into my life?" and "God, have You lost Your love for me?" But God is careful to remind us in His Word that *nothing* can separate us from His love and triumph for us in Christ Jesus. And that includes trouble.

A third truth for trouble is that *no trouble we are experiencing means an end to His love and care. If we look carefully, we will always find God and His love there.* It is simply impossible for the God and Father of our Lord Jesus Christ to be anything but a father to His children. His love remains. His love means action for our good—done in just the right way and at just the right time.

TRIUMPH OVER TROUBLE BY TRUSTING CHRIST

Every trouble we face in life comes as an invitation to triumph over it by trusting God in Christ. This invitation is received by heeding Jesus' command to stop being troubled by trouble and answer His call to trust *the God we cannot see* in spite of *the trouble we do see*. It is an invitation to all who trust Christ for eternal life to also trust Him in the face of life's great troubles.

Six months after Hugh Latimer and Nicholas Ridley died at the stake, Thomas Cranmer found himself in that same awful place. But he came by a very different route.

Like Latimer and Ridley, he was committed to his Protestant faith in Catholic England at a time when that was quite dangerous. Unlike them, he rose to the highest position in the Church of England, becoming the first Protestant Archbishop of Canterbury. He loved his comfortable life of quiet scholarship. Like all of us, he feared for the loss of his life.

Unlike Latimer and Ridley, Cranmer's faith wavered in the face of trouble. The man who had successfully steered the Church of England through the many turbulences of the Reformation and had given England *The Great Bible* in 1538, the *Book of Common Prayer* (1552) and the Articles of the Church of England ultimately found himself humiliated in the Bocardo prison in Oxford. From there, he watched Latimer and Ridley as they were burned at the stake. Some believe he may have been compelled to witness their deaths personally.

But two-and-a-half years of prison, badgering by hostile interrogators and sheer loneliness finally induced Cranmer to sign a document in which he recanted and denounced his cherished beliefs. His confidence in his faith had seemingly been crushed. In exchange for the end of his trouble, for the promise of his life and freedom, the broken man had given away his signature and more. It was the capitulation of one of the greatest living Protestant leaders—and it was an extraordinary victory for Queen Mary.

But the victory was short-lived. Mary's personal hatred for Cranmer was such that even though she had received his recantation, she insisted on seeing him burn anyway. Thus, Cranmer's trouble did not go away. Instead, it got worse.

The execution was held on the 21st of March, 1556. Cranmer was allowed to preach before a massive crowd to publicize his recantation. There, in the university church of St Mary's, he did something no one expected. He found, again, the strength that comes from faith and chose triumph in the midst of his trouble.

He repented of all his sins—as he was supposed to do—but he ended by repenting of his greatest sin of all: the denial of the Protestant gospel that espoused the sole sufficiency of Christ for salvation. It was a very public moment. As to his forced recantation, he said: "And forasmuch as my hand offended in writing contrary to my heart, therefore my hand shall first be punished; for if I may come to the fire, it shall be first burned."

He was not able to get much further. Furious hands seized him and hurried him down Brasenose Lane and then to the very same spot where Latimer and Ridley had died. Bound with steel around his waist, the fire began to engulf him. Cranmer put his right hand directly in the approaching flame, and he cried out, "This hand hath offended."

"This," writes Archbishop Marcus Loane, "was recantation of a kind which none could undo; a Sign of Faith which no one could misread. His patience in torment, his courage in dying, won admiration even from hostile members of the crowd which looked on. He stood firmly in the same place, ringed with flame, lapped with fire; and stirred no more than the stake to which he was bound, only lifting up his eyes and crying so long as his voice would allow, 'Lord Jesus, receive my spirit!' "

Here the command of Christ and His call were obeyed and received. This is great triumph in the midst of great trouble made real (at last) by great faith! And this is what Christ has for all who are His, who hear Him and believe Him when He says in troubled times, "In this world you will have trouble, but be of good cheer for I have overcome the world," so "Stop letting your hearts be troubled. Keep on believing in God, keep on believing also in Me."

His command and His call are for you! By faith, there is triumph in troubled times. ⟨꧁꧂⟩

Marcus Loane, *Masters of the English Reformation* (London: Church Book Room Press, 1954), 240.

Godly Leadership
(Exodus 18:8-23)

REV. DR. LARRY WAYNE ELLIS

Pilgrim Baptist Church
San Mateo, California

John Maxwell is a guru on leadership who has written several best-selling books on the subject. John is on television and radio, and he is the CEO of his own company. When asked to describe "leadership" in one word, he responded without hesitation that "leadership is influence. We all lead someone at some time." So, the question is, are we giving bad or good leadership or influence? Charles Barkley, the Hall of Fame NBA player, once shouted to the world that he was absolutely not a role model. It turned out that he was right.

Our nation is wrapped up in a presidential race that is dead even. The Democratic candidate Obama is running on the platform that leadership will bring change, while the Republican candidate McCain is running on the platform of leadership proven over time. (By the way, your vote will not count if you do not cast it, so please vote.) But what about godly leadership? What does God look for in a leader? What kind of leader would get our Lord's vote? It is His vote that "really" counts. Our vote is important but temporal; His vote is eternal and therefore permanent.

GOD'S LEADERS REMEMBER WHERE THEY'VE COME FROM

Moses had led the million-plus assembly of Hebrew ex-slaves to a location where they would be stationed for a while. At that time Jethro came to meet him, bringing Moses' wife Zipporah and his sons Gershom and Eliezer. (The people of God should understand divine timing. Nothing just happens to the child of God. There are no such things as accidents, coincidence, happenstance, fate or luck. God is in full control. The Lord orders the steps of the righteous [Psalm 37:23]). Jethro came by divine assignment, bringing Moses' wife and children for a family reunion. Moses, the greatest figure in the Old Testament as a prophet, priest and miracle worker, had been on the cutting edge of liberation, but now God wanted him to balance his life. In essence, God was saying, "Moses, I know you can walk through water, but let me see if you'll take out the trash! Receive your family and take them home."

I need to speak into the life of some parent or spouse. God knows that you can work a miracle in the workplace, but how are you handling your business at home? A son or daughter may be a queen or king on the campus but will not obey when they come home.

Moses began to tell his father-in-law all that God had done and was still doing: "It all started with a bush that was on fire but did not burn up. God called me to liberate His people from Egypt. I have done miracles of deliverance, protection, provision, power and presence. I led them across the Red Sea. God used me to sweeten bitter water with a tree. That is not all: Water gushed out of a rock. That is not all: Manna was sent from heaven. That is not all: Meat came down from heaven, and the healing of all manner of disease broke forth."

It is so easy for the blessed brother and sister to get amnesia about the past when the present is filled with prosperity. Now, do not misunderstand me on this point. I am not saying that you need to keep your mind on your past. However, do not ever forget the place from where the Lord has brought you.

My point is this: We all have had help on our way to get where we are now. God had sent Jethro to Moses at this opportune time. Thank God for His perfect timing! Jethro was there to remind the mighty Moses that a few years earlier he was a fugitive wanted for capital murder in Egypt. It was not too long ago that he came to Midian broke, hungry and in the unemployment line. Jethro did not intend to throw Moses' past into his face, but he just wanted to remind him that he was given a hand up. Jethro had given him a job, a camel to ride and free rent. He then gave him his daughter in marriage and paid for the bachelor party, the wedding and the honeymoon. In essence, Jethro said, "Moses, now is not the time to get amnesia."

One of the tragedies of this hour in history is that so many of us have forgotten from whence we have come. We did not always have what we have, drive what we drive and live where we live. We now get an attitude when God asks something of us. We need to remember that there was a time when we laid ourselves down before the altar every Sunday, praying that we would make it through one more week!

Maybe you have moved across the country. Things are going well. You adapt to the culture of your present location. Your parents come to visit, and you take them around to show how well you are doing. How modern you have become throwing off those old-fashioned mores! Your parents just take it all in and say nothing. On their way to the airport, they speak to you about it: "Dear, we are so proud of all of your accomplishments and achievements, but we did not raise you to live the way you are now living. The children are now talking back to you, and you ask their permission before you make a decision. What you feel like doing is not the way you were taught. We cannot tell you what to do, but you know better." Can anyone relate?

GOD'S LEADERS WELCOME MENTORING

Moses needed Jethro to come into his life as a mentor. (All leaders need someone to pour into their lives because they all need help.)

Jethro was on divine assignment. He observed Moses' daily work schedule, noticing that he left home early in the morning and came home late in the evening.

Jethro's insights:

What are you doing to the people? (Exodus 18:14)

- Doing God's work all alone.
- Working unreasonably long hours.
- What you are doing is not good (wise).
- You will wear out or fade away and die!

Instead,

- Teach the people how to walk before God.
- Teach them how to work for God (Exodus 18:20).
- Provide able men to assist you in leading.
- Teach them to use their gifts.
- Moses, you handle the weightier matters.
- Appoint others to handle the daily duties.

Moses' response:

- People come to me to inquire of God.
- I make known to them the statutes of God.
- It is my calling.

GODLY LEADERS TEACH
THEIR CONGREGATIONS TO MINISTER

Godly leadership, whether it is in the home, community, workplace or campus, is invaluable. We are called of God to pour into others by leading them to a place of maturity so their dependence is not on us.

A pastor should love his congregation too much to allow his people to settle for mediocrity, instead encouraging their personal growth and development. When a leader does everything for the people, it cripples the congregation. My pastor is always around, so you can call him 24/7. Yet, Joel Gregory said that the minister who is always available is not worth much when he is available. Second Timothy 2:1-2 says, "Thou therefore, my son, be strong in the grace that is in Christ Jesus. And the things thou hast heard of me among many witnesses, the same commit to faithful men, who shall be able to teach others also." Moreover, the apostle Paul says, "Those things that you have both learned, and received, and heard, and seen in me, do: and the God of peace will be with you" (Phil. 4:9).

It is a simple yet effective plan. Once God has helped you, then pass it on. The helped must one day become helpers! Jethro says it like this: "Teach the congregation to do ministry. Tell them to get their R's in place:

- Right person;
- Right place;
- Right Spirit;
- Right reason; and
- Right season."

Some have been blessed with the capacity to oversee thousands, some hundreds, some fifties and some tens. Some have a larger capacity than others. Some people have ten talents, some five and others only one. Yet, God does not bless on the basis of the size of your gift, but on the purity of your motive. Whatever is right, God will pay.

Jethro commits this work to able men, but today, should we allow only men to have the responsibilities?

- Sisters in Christ can bring their tithes but in some churches cannot count the money.
- Sisters in Christ can sweep around the pulpit but in some churches are not allowed to stand in the pulpit.
- Sisters in Christ can bake the communion bread, wash the cups and set the table up but in some churches cannot serve communion.
- Sisters in Christ can carry a boy child in her womb for nine months, raise him and put him through college but in some churches are not allowed to teach men.

Instead, I heard Paul say that your gift should make a way for you. Let us build congregations where love abides. Let us build families where the Holy Spirit has sway. I want to preach freedom today. Set the children free. Set the women free. Set the men free. Set the pastor free to pray, plan and preach! **You cannot do everything, but you can do something the Lord expects you to.**

GODLY LEADERS RECOGNIZE THAT MINISTRY IS A SHARED EXPERIENCE

The Exodus story is God's way of demonstrating that bondage of any kind is out of divine order, but it has more to say to us than that. It informs us that ministry is a shared experience. The post-modern paradigm of the pastor holding a celebrity status did not work for Moses, and it will not work for us today. The "thing" that we are doing today is still not good. What is this "thing"? We are making celebrities out of our pastors because we are star struck. We have reduced ministry from giving God glory to cheerleading for our "bishop." Thus, the congregation is judged by the success of membership and status of the preacher.

The National Basketball Association (NBA) is obsessed with finding the next Michael Jordan. Some newcomer is crowned before even walking on a court! Will it be Kobe of the Lakers? Or will it be LeBron of Cleveland? The church of Jesus Christ is not far behind. Who will be the next Billy Graham? Will it be T.D. Jakes, Joel Osteen or perhaps Rick Warren? The Center for Disease Control may need to name a disease specific to Christians: "celebrity-itis." We must regain the concept of the biblical call to each member to use his/her gifts in ministry. We admit that we are not equal in gifts or spiritual growth, but we are equal in grace!

In Matthew 25:14-30, we read about the parable of the talents. May I take the liberty to exchange the word "talent" for "gift" to make my point? One was given five gifts (talents). Another was given two and still another only one. Each steward was to do business until the master returned. Upon the return of the master, each was called to give an accounting of their "work." The one with five gained five more. The one with two gained two more. However, the one with only one gift (talent) buried it out of fear. The latter was judged severely.

What might our Lord decide concerning our use of gifts (talents)? Might it be our responsibility to re-employ the saints to go to work using their own gifts? It might be the pastor's charge to lead the people to get off the sidelines of ministry and go to work in God's vineyard. Whatever our capacity, it is born of grace. Whether we possess five gifts, two or just one, we need to use them to the glory of God! Second Corinthians 9:8 says that "God is able to make all grace abound toward us having sufficiency in all things lacking nothing." In the Body of Christ, there is no place for comparison, competition or self-congratulation! Grace is enough.

- Grace is sufficient.
- Grace watched over us last night.
- Grace met us this morning.
- Grace introduced us to Jesus.
- Grace informed us of the Holy Spirit.
- Grace placed us in the body of Christ.
- Grace sent Jesus into the world.
- Grace led him to Calvary.
- Grace has brought us safe thus far.
- Grace will make our dying bed.
- Grace will lead us home to bright glory.
- Grace will let us hear "well done."

As the hymn says, "Amazing grace, how sweet the sound/That saved a wretch like me/I once was lost, but now am found/Was blind but now I see!" Grace is enough! ❦

The Inconspicuous God: Finding God in Every Scene of Life
(Psalm 23; John 14:1-3)

ᴄᴄ❦ᴅ

PASTOR LEROY HILL JR.

Ebenezer Baptist Church
Portsmouth, Virginia

A former educator and educational administrator, I have taught on the middle school, high school and college levels. I am a fan of intrigue and mystery as it relates to teaching and learning. While serving as an elementary school administrator a few years ago, I came across a magazine for elementary students that I had used years ago as a student myself. *Highlights for Children* is a magazine of wholesome fun dedicated to helping children develop their basic skills and knowledge, creativity, ability to think and reason, sensitivity to others, high ideals and worthy ways of living. One of the main attractions for me is the "Hidden Pictures" section, which contains a picturesque scene like a ball game, a farm or a country diner. In each of these scenes are pictures of different objects or people hidden within the scene. The task for the student is to find the hidden items. Some of the objects are easy to find, but others are not so readily noticeable. The easy objects are obvious to the seeker because they stand out in the picture. The other items, which are not as apparent to the seeker, are certainly there, but are so creatively blended into the scene that it requires a little extra effort and focus in order to find them.

I discovered several years ago that God is like the "Hidden Pictures" section in the *Highlights* magazine. There are times when God can be so easily found in the scenes of our lives. However, there are also times in our lives when we think that maybe He is not with us. God doesn't seem so readily apparent; He's not easily noticeable. In these moments of our lives, God has become the inconspicuous God. To be sure, however, He is there! We may not see or feel Him like we are used to, but He is still there. In these times, He has so creatively blended Himself into the scenic realities of our lives that it requires a little extra effort and spiritual focus in order to discover that He has been there all the time.

The inconspicuous God is the God who is always *in* the scenes, *on* the scenes and *behind* the scenes of our lives. How wonderful it is to see God and discover Him so obviously or conspicuously moving in our lives—working with us, for us and around us. More wonderful, however, it is to discover God when we have thought, "It's over," "The goose is cooked" or "It's 11:59 p.m.," only to realize that God was there all the time. He was just conspicuously inconspicuous. Like the word search puzzles, the words are there! They may be placed diagonally, horizontally or vertically. They may be placed in the puzzle forwards or backwards, but the listed words are there—in the puzzle! You have to seek them in order to find them. Long ago, the Lord said to the prophet Jeremiah, "You will seek Me and find Me, when you search for Me with all your heart. I will be found by you, says the Lord" (Jer. 29:13-14a). God can be found!

The 23rd Psalm and John 14 frequently show up together on funeral programs as the Scriptures to be read for comfort, and I have read them at scores of funerals. I have preached these texts at funerals and at other times during my 25 years of preaching and two decades of pastoring. It was not until my unfortunate yet glorious privilege to eulogize both my father, from the 23rd Psalm, and my mother, from John 14:1-3, that I gained this revelation of the inconspicuous God. I found Him in two scenic realities of my life. I lost my father during a very difficult time in my life and ministry when he was assisting me greatly through my trials. In fact, two weeks before he died, he advised me to do whatever it took to restore my family and save my ministry. Three weeks after he died, I applied his advice and restored my family and the integrity of my ministry. When it seemed as if God wasn't there clearly, clearly He was there.

While I was trying to find a word from the Lord to preach a celebratory message about my father, my mother shared with me (out of the blue) some tidbits of my father's personal struggle with God's calling on his life. He never fully surrendered to the call to preach the gospel, at least publicly or officially. However, he was masterful with the Scriptures, and he could sing a church congregation happy with his sultry Sam Cooke, Otis Redding-like voice. Anyway, my father once told my mother that, if and when he did finally surrender to preach, his first sermon would be from Psalm 23. "Bam!" as Emeril the chef would say, there it was. On November 29, 1997, I eulogized my father with this subject, "My Father's First Sermon: The 23rd Psalm." I found my God in the text in ways that I had not seen or heard, but He was there waiting for me to find Him.

Again, while meditating and searching for celebratory words to eulogize my mother, I came across some of her Disney collection. My mother (who had a passion for children and ran a daycare for many years) was a true Disney fan. She raised her children and grandchildren to appreciate Disney as well. John 14:1-3 was my text of choice for her eulogy, and the story of Snow White and the Seven Dwarfs was my illustration and celebratory conclusion. I had never realized that there were so many spiritual undertones and overtones, as well as basic biblical and theological principles, in Snow White that are applicable to our lives.

My, my, my, did God allow me to discover Him behind the scenes of Snow White and the Upper Room discourse of Jesus to His disciples in ways I had never experienced! (Stick a pin here, I will come back to it later.) On January 14, 2006 I eulogized my precious mother with this subject, "Real Life Behind the Scenes."

A thought occurred to me one day to bump these two Scriptural jewels together to see if I could find God afresh in these texts in ways that I had never known Him. You guessed it. I discovered through spiritual focus and insight that God truly is the inconspicuous God who can be found in all the scenes of life. Follow me now as I take you on my journey of discovery. It is my hope and prayer that as we journey, you too will find God revealing Himself to you in ways that you have not felt, seen or heard before—until now.

The Book of Psalms is a part of that wonderful division of the Old Testament called the Writings. The Book of Psalms, the hymnal of the Israelites, is the most often-quoted Old Testament book found in New Testament writings. This book is comprised of songs that express praises to God, which is fittingly so, because the Hebrew title for the Book of Psalms is *tehillim*, meaning "praises." The Book of Psalms is composed by multiple authors with multiple themes and categories, such as penitential psalms (feeling regret or sorrow for sins; repentance), hallel psalms (praise), imprecatory psalms (to invoke evil on), messianic psalms (relating to the Messiah) and songs of ascents or degrees ("going up" to the Temple).

Some 73 of these psalms were written by David, the king of Israel. It is no wonder why he is tagged with the nickname "sweet singer," or "sweet psalmist" of Israel. It is God's very own testimony that David was a man after His heart (Acts 13:22; Psalm 89:20; 1 Samuel 13:14). The 23rd Psalm is nestled within the first of the five smaller books of Psalms. Book I contains Psalms 1-41; they are called the Yahweh psalms because there is an attraction, an emotional awareness, a keen insight, an affinity, a central use and an appreciation, or praise for the divine name of Yahweh.

Yahweh, the personal covenant name of God whose meaning was first explained to Moses (Ex. 3), emphasizes the living presence of God with, and for, His people. It was as Yahweh that God released His people from slavery in Egypt. It was as Yahweh that He parted the Red Sea, provided Israel with manna as their daily bread and shattered the power of the Canaanites before Joshua's armies. It was as Yahweh that God settled the Israelites in the Promised Land, gave them the Law to live by and promised to bless them. It is Yahweh—the ever-present, ever–faithful, and ever-caring God—whom we meet in the Psalms. And it is through the Psalms that we sense that God is Yahweh for us.

The 14th chapter of John is the classic text that many refer to as the cure for a troubled heart. Jesus clearly saw that His disciples needed some help with the news He had just revealed to them. He was going to leave them, one of them was going to betray Him, and Peter was going to deny Him. Yes, they needed some help after such a bombshell like that exploded in their souls. His words of comfort, encouragement and hope in this chapter were the antidote for their troubled hearts. Jesus reveals more about the Father (23 times) in His valedictory discourse in the 14th chapter than He does of Himself or the Holy Spirit, and this is significant.

THE SHEPHERD SCENE

In our texts, there are scenes for discovery. In the 23rd Psalm, often called the "Shepherd Psalm," we are exposed to three scenes that the psalmist depicts for us. The first scene is the shepherd scene (vv. 1-4), in which the divine Shepherd loves, leads, feeds, tends, protects and cares for His sheep (the psalmist). We clearly see God in this scene, as the psalmist declared Him to be his Shepherd. Yahweh is the ultimate caregiver, where His hand—as the late Rev. Dr. E. K. Bailey would say, the *Jehovistic hand*—of His possession, provision, patience, peacefulness, preservation, presence and protection is clearly active in the life of His sheep. No wonder that this is a psalm of praise and celebration. The Shepherd is so active in the life of His sheep that the sheep has no lack: "I shall not want."

What makes this scene so interesting is the verb tense. All of the verbs in this scene are in the imperfect tense, suggesting that the Shepherd is continuing to act, or repeating His activity in the life of His sheep. Let me say it another way using the text: "He [continuously] makes me lie down...He [continuously] leads me...He [continuously] restores my soul... He [continuously] leads me in the paths..." Are you with me? This Shepherd protects, guides and comforts His sheep in dark, dangerous places. He is some kind of Shepherd. David is saying, "Because God is my Shepherd, I have no need to worry." Jesus is saying in the Upper Room scene at the Last Supper, "Fellows, don't be troubled, agitated or anxious in your hearts. You believe in God! You know, the One David said is the Shepherd, and in Him there is no lack. Yes, you believe in God or (in the imperative voice) Believe in God! He is the divine Shepherd. Believe also in Me! I am the Good Shepherd, the One who is all that you need. What more could you want or ask?" Certainly, He is Yahweh God *in* the scenes of our lives.

THE BANQUET SCENE

The second scene is the host or banquet scene (v. 5). Verse five depicts a guest at a banquet of an unusual kind. The guest attends this banquet (presumably held for him) as pictured in the verse, and his enemies are allowed to be present. Now, that is strange. It was the custom during those days to eat, commune and fellowship with those who were considered a part of one another. While I was reading this passage from the Tanakh Translation (a Jewish Society publication of the Old Testament), the scene became vividly clear. The Tanakh translates verse 5a, "You spread a table for me in full view of my enemies." This suggests that God the Host has a banquet for His own, where He luxuriously provides a bountiful spread on the banquet table and then allows the enemies to only look at the blessings but not partake. It has been suggested that this is symbolic of God's protective care over His own in the midst of a vicious, cruel, wicked, unrighteous and antagonistic world chaotically governed by the Devil and his demons. Not only does Yahweh the Host spread a table, but He also anoints His guest with oil, as was the custom for honored guests in the Middle East. The anointing oil was a refreshing, aromatic fragrance mixed with olive oil to prepare the guest for fellowship at the table. Oil is one of the symbols of the Holy Spirit. He is our anointing (1 John 2:20a, 27a) and our refreshing who prepares us for right fellowship at the Lord's table. In the words of my pastor, mentor and grandfather, the Rev. Dr. H. A.

Walker, "He is the great God from Zion!" What a picture! Yahweh the gracious Host prepares a sumptuous spread for His children, refreshes and anoints them for banquet fellowship, while the satanic and the demonic minions can only get an eyeful of the goodness of God. Jesus, Himself a Host, said, "I go to prepare a place for you… I will come again and receive you…" (v. 2). According to Revelation 19:7-9, there is another banquet that will take place with God and His people. This banquet is the marriage supper of the Lamb! Again, there will be no satanic or demonic participation. Clearly, we see our God who is *on* the scene blessing our lives while the enemies around us can only look at what God is doing with us, in spite of all they try to do to us.

THE HEAVENLY HOME SCENE

There is a third and final scene that is placed before us in this 23rd Psalm by David, the praise and worship leader of the Old Testament. This is the heavenly home scene. Here the picture is of the saint's confident assurance of perpetual fellowship of a heavenly kind. Notice here that this scene reveals no threat of danger, nor is there any satanic adversarial presence. Evil, danger and death are completely absent. His assurance is based on two divine escorts as rearguards in pursuit of his life until he gets to his eternal home.

The sixth verse mentions, "Surely goodness and mercy…", which are covenant blessings from Yahweh. These are twin graces that pursue His own throughout life—all the way to the house of the Lord, the eternal dwelling place. In other words, God has got our back until we get home. Jesus promises His disciples a prepared place for a prepared people. The Lord says there is plenty of room, mansions and dwelling places—like contemporary apartments or townhouses—in His Father's house. We too, can have confident assurance throughout our lives (or in the Hebrew, "for length of days") because God has granted to us opportunities for intimate fellowship with Him now and for all eternity. What a blessed assurance we have when we can see God *behind* the scenes of our lives.

THE GOD WHO IS THERE

Some of you may be saying, "Preacher, I'm with you and have followed you thus far. However, could you please tell me how what you have previously said has to do with the inconspicuous God? So far, I have seen God clearly *in* the scene, *on* the scene and *behind* the scene. So where is your evidence for an inconspicuous God who is always in all the scenes of life?" In the words of the elder sages, "I'm glad you asked."

Let's revisit our scenes again, in order that the inconspicuous God may be found in all the scenes. As you may recall, King David revealed three scenes to us in the 23rd Psalm: 1) the Shepherd scene, 2) the banquet scene and 3) the heavenly home scene. Obviously, we see the Lord as divine Shepherd, Host and Homeowner.

Lest we move too fast, let's look carefully with some effort and spiritual detection. In verse one, we find the Lord: Stop! He is Yahweh ("I AM WHO I AM"), whose name is also transliterated as Jehovah. He is the personal God who reveals Himself to man. Often, when the revelation occurs, the place of God's self-disclosure is named to memorialize His revelation of Himself and how He revealed Himself to humanity in that place. To David, He is Shepherd or Jehovah-Rohi, *The Lord is my Shepherd*. David continued in this scene, "I shall not want": that's provision. He is Jehovah-Jireh, *The Lord will provide*. In verse two, "He makes me lie down in green pastures and leads me to quiet waters of rest": that's peace. He is Jehovah-Shalom, *The Lord is peace*. "He restores my soul": that's healing. He is Jehovah-Rapha, *The Lord who heals*. "He guides me in the paths of righteousness." He is Jehovah-Tsidkenu, *The Lord our righteousness*. "Even though I walk through the valley... I fear no evil; for You are with me": that's presence. He is Jehovah-Shammah, *The Lord is there*.

Did you see Him? Yes! He was there all the time. He was in the scene. He was on the scene. He was behind the scene. He was not readily noticeable in the scene, but He was there. That is why I call Him the Inconspicuous God. If you keep looking, you will find Him to be the God of all comfort: He is there. If you look again, you may see Him as the Eternal and Everlasting God. Look further still, and He will be a banner of protection, a sanctifier, an ever-present help and a refuge in times of trouble. Do you see Him? He is there. He is in all the scenes of our lives. He did say, "If you seek Me you will find Me, if you search for Me with all your heart" (Jer. 29:13).

Yet, there is still more. Jesus is there. He is the Chief Shepherd, the Good Shepherd and the Great Shepherd of the sheep. He is the Prince of peace and the Lord of peace. He is our peace. He is our righteousness. He is Immanuel and the fragrant offering. He is there, He is there and He is there! Jesus is salvation, eternal life and the way to the Father's house. Jesus says to us, "Don't be troubled, agitated or aggravated (a divine prohibition), but believe in God (you know, the God who is always in the scene, on the scene and behind the scenes of our lives). He is the inconspicuous God. Furthermore, Jesus says to believe also in Him (a divine prescription). Like the Father, Jesus can be conspicuously inconspicuous. He is always there, working in the scene, working on the scene and working behind the scenes of our lives (Rom. 8:28).

Let me encourage you. No matter what is going on in your life, whether it be celebration or frustration, stop long enough to find out where God is in that scene. As we have discovered, He is always somewhere involved in our lives. David said that Yahweh was his Shepherd, banquet Host and heavenly Homeowner. Jesus said our hearts don't have to be troubled in our times of trial. He said for us to have faith in God and trust Him as well. David had confident assurance about goodness and mercy pursuing him to the house of the Lord and dwelling there forever. Jesus said He is working on our dwelling places right now and will come back to take us to be with Him, in His Father's house for all eternity. I eagerly await with confident expectation to see my heavenly home. Until then, I will keep on looking to find the Inconspicuous God. I know without a doubt He is in all the scenes of life.

"LOVE'S FIRST KISS"

Remember, we stuck a pin in this sermon earlier. Pull it out now, as we conclude this journey. I shared with you earlier that I am a fan of mystery and intrigue when it comes to teaching and learning. I believe that personal discovery deepens the learning experience and impacts the learner. Many times in our lives, there are truths waiting to be discovered by us. They surround us. We only need to take a moment to look for truth in different ways. That is what I discovered when bringing two classic "funeral texts" together to find God afresh. What I found is celebration and a confident expectation—the joy of hope.

Then, the question came to me: Why should I look for the inconspicuous God as I journey toward this life's end? Jesus spoke to me from the text: "And if I go… I will come again…" Now, as I believe it, Jesus did go. I do believe He will come again. My answer became clear to me as I pondered on yet another question: What do I do between His going and His coming? For most New Testament preachers of the gospel of Jesus Christ, this is the proverbial "softball." Conspicuously, we see the Great Commission standing on the back side of the Gospel of Matthew (Matt. 28:18-20). We see also the succinct "table of contents" for the Book of Acts and the strategic plan for the New Testament church in Acts 1:8. There are many other obvious references that I could mention. However, the Holy Spirit tugged at my heart and said, "If He can be found in all places, by all means look for Him in all places." Here is where the story of Snow White and the Seven Dwarfs helped me. I recalled a principle I was taught by my systematic theology professor Dr. Kirkpatrick (while attending Southwestern Baptist Theological Seminary). There is simplicity in complexity, and there is profundity in simplicity. This movie is simplistic, yet it profoundly helps to answer the question, "What do we do between His going and coming?"

Surprisingly, this story is full of hope and expectation of a better life—a free and happy life. Snow White appears singing a song of hope at the wishing well: "I'm wishing for the one I love to find me today." Do you love Him? Can you see Him? Paul said it like this, "Christ in you the hope of glory" (Col. 1:27). Snow White is forced into the forest due to circumstances beyond her control. She falls asleep and awakens to find many eyes upon her. She befriends these furry and feathery creatures as she continues her journey. While walking in the forest, she asks her newfound friends a question: "What do you do when things go wrong?" Then, she answers, "Sing a song." She sings to the delight of her friends as they discover a cottage. They go in the cottage and see that it is all cluttered with junk. The reason for the junk is a no-brainer. Seven men lived in that place. Immediately, she begins to clean the place with the help of her friends. She sings yet another song, "Whistle while you work… working together to get the job done." Snow White meets and befriends the seven little men: Happy, Sleepy, Sneezy, Dopey, Grumpy, Bashful and Doc.

Life appears to be going well for Snow White. She is so filled with hope and joy that she sings what would become her swan song: "Someday my prince will come and take me to his castle." (Can't you see Him? Can't you feel Him? He is there. He is in the scenes and the songs of our lives.) However, she is victimized by evil through a deceitful plot by a wicked Queen. Snow White eats a poisoned apple and falls into a death sleep. No one could help her—not her furry and feathery friends nor her seven, little, lovable and loyal companions. Snow White's only hope is to be cured by "Love's First Kiss," that is, the kiss of a loving prince. They place Snow White in a glass case and look on in despair, as if there is no hope. (Great God from Zion, there are many who are dead [asleep] in their trespasses and sins, and their only hope is "Love's First Kiss" from a loving prince. Come on, say His name! Jesus! He is the inconspicuous God.)

Well, one day the prince came. He was riding on his white horse, dressed in his royal regalia and singing his "one song, about one love, and about one heart." The prince in his royal dignity comes to the cottage, dismounts his horse, goes inside and lifts the glass, kisses Snow White the princess and she awakens. The prince takes Snow White to his radiant castle, and they live happily ever after. Oh, friend, oh saint, can you see it? Can you see Him? He is there. I am in the scene. You are in the scene. We are in the scene. The church is in the scene. The world is in the scene, but Jesus is in the scene, on the scene and behind the scene of our lives, for Jesus is always there. I like how Bertha Mae Lillenas said it in the last stanza of her hymn "Jesus Is Always There":

"Lo, I am with you always," is written,
God will not fail to answer our prayer;
Trusting His word we rest in His promise—
Jesus is always there.

CHORUS
Never a burden that He doth not carry,
Never a sorrow that He doth not share;
Whether the days may be sunny or dreary,
Jesus is always there.
Amen.

Richards, Lawrence O., *The Bible Readers Companion*, electronic ed. (Wheaton : Victor Books, 1991; published in electronic form by Logos Research Systems, 1996), S. 349.

The God-Breathed Word
(2 Timothy 3:16-17)

c⋅C✹Ɔ⋅ɔ

REV. DR. CLAYBON LEA JR.

Mount Calvary Baptist Church
Fairfield, California

From the millions of books available today—including the historical, the governmental, the legal, the educational, the poetic, the scientific, the psychological and the philosophical—there is one that rules and reigns supreme, and that is the Holy Bible. As a matter of fact, it reigns in such a way that no other book has ever sold more copies. No book has been more widely distributed than the Holy Bible. No book has been translated into as many languages and dialects as the Holy Bible because it has no peer and no literary superior. What other book offers so much to so many to all generations, nations, ethnic groups and races upholding the Christian faith? Unlike any other book, the Holy Bible offers a pardon to the prisoner, assurance to the anxious, blessings to the burdened, help for the helpless, hope for the hopeless, comfort to the lonely and deliverance to the bound. There is no other book like the Bible.

There is no law book; there is no storybook; there is no record book; there is no history book; there is no cookbook; there is no date book; there is not even a checkbook that can offer what this book offers. The Holy Bible is unique in a myriad ways, to say the least. God's Word sets itself apart from all others by what it promises; it can and does deliver. It sets itself apart from all others by what it prescribes; it can and does fulfill. It sets itself apart from all others because what it demands, it can and does provide. It sets itself apart from all others because what it proclaims, it can and does confirm. It sets itself apart from all others because what it declares, it can and does defend without the need and assistance of any defense attorney. There is no book like the Holy Bible. It does not require the approval of humanity nor the support of politicians. It does not require the patronage of historians nor the endorsements of the press. It does not even rely upon the interpretation of the commentaries, the apologetics of the saints or even the backing of the clergy in order to stand. The Bible stands all by itself: *Sola Scriptura.*

In 1788, Voltaire said, "One hundred years from my day, there will not be a Bible in the earth except one that is looked upon by an antiquarian curiosity seeker." History tells us that a century later, a Bible society was being set up and established to distribute Bibles in Voltaire's home. On that day, we discover that Great Britain paid $500,000 for the *Codex Sinaiticus*, an ancient copy of the Bible. Voltaire's first edition of his work sold that same day for just 11 cents. There is no book like the Bible.

While penning these words to his son in the ministry, Timothy, the apostle Paul reminded him that many had begun to fall away from the faith. As a result, he wanted to encourage and admonish Timothy to remain true to the Scriptures. He urged Timothy to always remember that the Scriptures were not new to him. Timothy had learned them at the knees of his mother and grandmother, Eunice and Lois. He discovered at an early age that the Scriptures were able to make one wise unto salvation. Therefore, the apostle Paul told Timothy to make sure that he remained true to the Word of Almighty God.

In these verses, note how Paul intimated that Timothy had already apparently experienced and heard enough to confirm the reliability of the Scriptures in his own life. Consequently, Paul was able to admonish Timothy to stay true to the Scriptures. He reminded him of the words that God brings to our attention in 2 Timothy 3:16-17: "All Scripture is God-breathed and is useful for teaching, rebuking, correcting, and training in righteousness so that the man of God may be thoroughly equipped for every good work."

WHAT MAKES THE BIBLE RELIABLE?

The relevant question is not, "Is the Bible reliable?" but "What makes the Bible reliable?" What makes the Bible the most reliable book to dictate our doctrine and our duty, our belief and our behavior? Paul answers that question succinctly. The first thing that he says, using the first of two verbs in this one sentence, is that the Bible is reliable because the Bible is God-breathed. What a statement this is: "All Scripture is God-breathed." That is to say, everything in the Bible, from Genesis to Revelation, is God-breathed. The Pentateuch, also called the Torah, is God-breathed. The Writings, also known as the wisdom literature, are God-breathed. The Major Prophets are God-breathed. The Minor Prophets are God-breathed. The Gospels are God-breathed. The Book of Acts is God-breathed. The General Epistles are God-breathed. The Pauline Epistles are God-breathed. The Apocalypse is God-breathed. "All Scripture is God-breathed."

When this verse says that "all Scripture is God-breathed," it suggests that the writers of holy writ inhaled the breath of God. Upon doing so, they gained knowledge of that which was to be written. They were then able to exhale the Word of God in spoken or written form. The picture is that as God spoke to them, God breathed into them. They inhaled the breath of God. They then exhaled the breath of God as the Word of God, true to what God said, without error.

The fact that God's Word is God-breathed suggests several things. *First, the Bible is inspired.* The fact that it is God-breathed means that the Bible is inspired in both the Hebrew and the Greek language, as well as the small amounts of Aramaic. *Inspired* denotes a forcible, conscious and thus intentional breathing into and breathing upon. According to William Evans in *Great Doctrines of the Bible*, inspiration as defined by Paul in this passage is "a strong conscious inbreathing of God into men qualifying them to give voice to truth." It is God speaking through men.

The central understanding is that as these men of God spoke and wrote, it was God who was literally speaking through them after having breathed into them. The fact that God's Word is God-breathed says that it is inspired. The words of the apostle Peter, in 2 Peter 1:20-21, corroborate the idea of God literally speaking through these men of God without their own idiosyncrasies tainting the purity of God's divine message. Peter says, "Above all, you must understand that no prophecy of Scripture came about by the prophet's own interpretation. For prophecy never had its origin in the will of man, but men spoke from God as they were carried along by the Holy Spirit." It is clear that God's Word is reliable because it is inspired.

The fact that the Bible is God-breathed not only suggests that it is inspired, but that it is *revelatory*. That which is revelatory is that which is revealing or has been revealed. It is fascinating that the Word of God is a revelation that keeps continuing to reveal. It was revealed to those to whom God spoke. Yet, every time we read God's Word, it reveals even more of what's already been revealed. It is revelatory.

Revelation suggests the act of God by which He directly communicates truth not known before to the human mind. Some might ask, "What is the difference between inspiration and revelation?" Revelation reveals, but inspiration releases. Revelation discovers, inspiration divulges. Revelation surprises, inspiration supervises. Revelation conceives, inspiration delivers. Revelation shows, inspiration tells. The Word of God reveals His truth about Himself as expressed through His Son, Jesus the Christ.

The fact that the Bible is God-breathed not only says that it is inspired and revelatory, but it is also *authoritative*. Why is it authoritative? It is authoritative because of its source. If it had simply come from men rather than through men, it could not be considered legitimately authoritative. It did not come from men, however. It came through men from God so that we might understand more about His Son. The Bible is authoritative because God is its author.

The biblical characters who chronicled God's inspired and revelatory message acknowledged God's authorship in their writings. In Exodus 32:16, Moses was very clear that the writings were the writings of God. Exodus 31:18 says that "the two tablets of the Testimony were written with the finger of God." Exodus 34:27 says, "The Lord said unto Moses, 'Write thou these words.' " First Chronicles 28:19 says, " 'All this,' said David, 'have I been made to understand in the writing from the hand of Jehovah.' " Isaiah 8:1 reads, "Moreover the Lord said unto me, 'Take thee a great scroll and write in it with a man's pen.' " Jeremiah's prophetic writing in 13:12 reads, "Therefore thou shall speak unto them this word, 'Thus sayeth the Lord God of Israel.' " In 1 Corinthians 14:37, Paul says, ". . .the things I write unto you are the commandments of the Lord." In Revelation 1:10-11, John was inspired to write these words: "On the Lord's Day, I was in the Spirit and I heard behind me a loud voice like a trumpet which said to me, 'Write on the scroll what you see.' " All I am trying to tell you is that the God-breathed Word has authority in the life of every believer because it's breathed from God.

THE BIBLE IS PROFITABLE

It is God-breathed so it is inspired, revelatory and authoritative, but there is another verb used here. The apostle says, "All scripture is God-breathed and is profitable." The second thing that we need to understand is that the Bible is profitable. Now the interesting thing is this: The Bible is profitable because it is God-breathed. Paul delineates several ways in which the God-breathed Word is profitable. He says it is useful and is profitable for teaching, rebuking, correcting and training in righteousness. I do not have time to unpack all of these, but allow me to cluster these four into two divisions. They are profitable, first of all, because the Bible is profitable for belief. Second, it is profitable for behavior. The first of the two clusters—doctrine, teaching and reproof—help us to understand how profitable the Scriptures are for belief. Theologian John Calvin said that "the Bible provides us with spectacles of faith, lenses of which we can look and understand the words and the intent of God's very heart." In essence, Paul says to Timothy, "You need to make certain, son, that you do not allow culture to dictate your belief."

We live in an age of post-modernity that challenges our belief systems. There was a theological apparatus that was created many years ago called the Wesleyan quadrilateral, which can be used as a grid of understanding: What is most authoritative, and what is it that informs our beliefs the most? Is it Scripture? Is it tradition? Is it experience? Is it history? What informs our belief system the most? If Scripture is not greater in impact than tradition, culture, experience and history, then we have a major problem.

We need the Scriptures. Tradition is fine. Experience is fine. History is fine. Ultimately, however, we need the Scriptures to inform what we believe and to justify why we believe it. Jaroslav Pelikan said in his history of the church that "what the church preaches and teaches about Jesus Christ from the Word of God, that is its doctrine." If we are not preaching and teaching out of the Word of God about Jesus Christ, then we have adopted a heretical gospel. The profitability of the Scriptures is that it informs us of what it is that we should believe and why we should believe it. Doctrinal teaching nourishes and develops our faith.

In *Stewards of the Story: The Task of Preaching*, Dr. James Earl Massey discusses five things that doctrine does functionally. First, it differentiates the church from the world. If we believe the same thing that the world believes, then there is no difference between the two of us. Second, doctrine provides a framework by which the church is able to understand and explain itself. Third, doctrine is necessary to illumine human experience. Fourth, doctrine offers true claims about our beliefs regarding our God. Finally, he suggested that doctrine functions to inform the church of its evangelical mission—to share Jesus Christ with the world—but we would not know that if it were not for the Scriptures.

William J. Carl III wrote in *The Concise Encyclopedia of Preaching* that "Christian doctrine is not identical with the proclamation of the gospel. Doctrine serves proclamation, enriches and enhances it, largely in a critical role, as a criterion for determining that what the church proclaims today is in harmony with scripture and its tradition, that it is truly human language about God and not about the latest spiritual trend or social ethical passion." In other words, what he was suggesting is that the gospel is enriched in such a way that it can inform and enhance our preaching and teaching so that it places upon us a "leash" that will keep us from veering too far from the Scriptures and adopting all kinds of belief that we would these days call syncretism: We are open to blend a little bit of this and a little bit of that and a little bit of the other.

I'm simply trying to say to you that the Bible is profitable because it helps us to understand what we ought to believe in doctrine, but also through reproof. Whenever an individual comes up with enormous un-biblical, de-contextualized theories about God, the Scriptures and life, we should be so saturated by this same God-breathed Word that we should be able to lovingly rebuke them. We should be able to suggest to them that while their theories sound good, they are not correct. If they are just repeating old wives' tales that have been passed down through the generation but are not in the Scriptures, we can reprove them lovingly so that they will not continue to uphold wrong beliefs that are not biblically grounded. Paul tells Timothy that he's got to make sure that he remains true to the Scriptures because of its doctrinal ability to reprove.

Then Paul says the Bible is not only profitable for belief, but also for behavior. Nothing can correct your behavior like the Word of God. The apostle says it is profitable for correcting and training in righteous-ness. I would submit to you that correction and training go hand in hand. I have two dogs which are Boxers. In the midst of the early years of training them to sit, stay and walk with me by my side, I had to cor-rect them. I had to train them not to get ahead of me and run away from me. When they got too far ahead, I had to pull back on the leash so that they would know to stay with me. When I told them to sit and they did not sit, I had to train them in a certain way. So it is with the Word of God, which will correct and train us to understand what we should and should not do as the children of Almighty God.

How many times have you come to church and heard a sermon or a lesson that convicted you about your behavior? Can you imagine the wild and riotous lifestyle you would live if it were not for the correcting and training power of God's Holy Word? Can you imagine how much sin you and I would still be engaged in, if it were not for the correcting and training facets of God's Holy Word? He says the Bible is profitable because it helps us in our behavior by correcting us and training us. It does not simply train us, however; it trains us in *righteousness*.

There is a disciplining facet of the Word that causes us to be developed and matured in things that are of God and not simply things that are of the church. In too many of our churches, we train people *in the church*, but we have not trained them *in righteousness*. So we as Baptists do not talk as much as we should about holiness. Instead, we leave it to some other denomination as if it were a deformational mandate that the Lord gave us, but it does not apply. Remember, however, that all Scripture is God-breathed. We must be trained in righteousness and the things of God so that our behavior reflects more and more of the image of the Lord Jesus Christ by the sanctifying work of the Holy Spirit and the transforming power of God's Word.

Paul says the Word is God-breathed and therefore profitable, but then he gives us a purpose clause to conclude this long sentence. He says the purpose of this God-breathed Word is profitable so that the man of God may be thoroughly equipped for every good work. Is the Bible reliable? The answers to that question are right there—that through the God-breathed Word we can be and are equipped thoroughly. Why did Paul not simply say, "so that the man of God may be equipped for every good work?" Why "thoroughly"? The apostle wanted us to understand that the Word of God is so reliable that it, in and of itself, is all that we need for all that we do. And everything that we need is in the Word of God so that we might be completely, absolutely—in every part and in every way—equipped, built up and given tools to accomplish every good work. Because the God-breathed Word is inspired, it is revelatory and authoritative. It's the God-breathed Word that is profitable: It is profitable for our belief and our behavior so that we may be thoroughly equipped and furnished for every good work.

STAND ON THE WORD OF GOD!

My friends, I don't know about you, but I'm determined to encourage everyone I know to be true to the Word of God. And if the church does not return fully and completely to the Word of God, then the world will go to hell in a handbasket. If we do not believe that the Word of God is reliable, then countless millions of people will be lost because of the Church's failure to believe. We have got to stand firm and tall on our convictions. Gordon C. Taylor says that we do not stand to argue our doubts but to present our convictions. If we do not have any convictions, we are like a tub that does not have any bottom to set on.

The Word of God and God reminds us that His Word is reliable, and because it comes from Him we need not wonder whether or not it will last. Numbers 23:19 says, "God is not a man that He should lie, nor the son of man that He should repent." That is why Isaiah was able to say that just like the rain and the dew that come down from the heavens and fall upon the earth do not return from whence it has come, so the Word of God will not return to Him void and will accomplish everything it will do what He says it will do (Isa. 55:11). In other words, God was saying through Isaiah that you can count on His Word. We have got to stand on the Word of God, every jot and tittle. On every vowel point, we have got to stand on the Word of God. On every penult and anti-penult in Greek, we have got to stand on the Word of God. We have got to make sure that we believe and proclaim that the Word is true. And you do know that the Bible declares that a whole lot of things are not going to last? But Jesus said, "Heaven and earth may pass away, but my Word will stand forever" (Matt. 24:35). That sounds like reliability to me, so I am going to press on and stand on the Word of God.

I was not there when the flowers first bloomed, but I believe the Word of God. I was not there when the birds sang their first song, but I believe the Word of God. I was not there when the bees made their first batch of honey, but I believe God's Word. I was not there when the lions roared for the first time, but I believe God's Word. I was not there when God made man in His own image and breathed into his nostrils the breath of life; but the Word says it, so I believe it. I was not there when Abraham at 100 and Sarah at 90 gave birth to their son Isaac; but the Bible says it, so I believe it. I was not there when the Israelites crossed the Sea of Reeds; but because the Bible says it, I believe it. I was not there when Elijah prayed down fire from heaven; but the Bible says it, so I believe it. I was not there when Jesus performed His first miracle at the wedding in Cana of Galilee; but the Bible says it, so I believe it. I was not there when He defied the law of mathematics by multiplying 2 x 5 and feeding over 5,000 men and women plus the disciples; but the Bible says it, so I believe it. And you know I was not there one Friday afternoon when they stretched Him wide and hung Him high and He died for my sins; but the Bible says it, so I believe it. I was not there when He descended down into the belly of the earth and led captivity captive; but the Bible says it, so I believe it. I was not there early Sunday morning when He arose with all power in His hands; but the Bible says it, so I believe it. I was not there when He showed His hands and side to His disciples, and said to Thomas, "If you do not believe, stick your hand in there." I do not know how it happened because I was not there; but the Bible says it, so I believe it. But I tell you what: I might not have been there for any of those things; but one glad morning when this life is over, I will be there when the trumpet sounds. The dead in Christ will rise, and we who are alive will be caught up to meet Him in the air. It has not happened yet; but it is in the Word, so I believe it. ⌀

William F. Carl III, "Doctrine," in *Concise Encyclopedia of Preaching,* eds. William H. Willimon and Richard Lisher (Louisville: Westminster John Knox, 1995), 102.

When You Are Feeling Down
(Psalm 42:1-11)

✦

REV. DR. RAYMOND MCDONALD II

St. John Baptist Church
Gary, Indiana

All of us have within us a God-shaped void—a void that only God can fill. Tragically, we deny this reality by attempting to control our own lives. Out of our rebellion and refusal to acknowledge God, we want our will, rather than God's will, to be done. We seek human, worldly power rather than the power of God's Spirit. We seek beauty rather than the One who creates both beauty and our ability to perceive it. We pursue a chemical high rather than a spiritual high. Rather than worshipping the creator, we worship the creation. Tragically, we worship that which is finite rather than the infinite. We prefer the transitory (that which is passing rather than that which is lasting); but in reality, this God-shaped void, this vacuum, that is within us can only be filled by God.

We live in an age of substitutes. Through modern science, man has come up with a substitute for just about every need. Modern medicine has substitute medications known as generics. Medical technology has even come up with a substitute for various parts of the human anatomy, including hair, teeth and legs. Cosmetology, through the aid of various cosmetics, has come up with substitute looks for the human face. Of all his substitute inventions, however, man cannot invent a substitute to fill the God-shaped void that is within him.

Contrary to the teachings of charismatic theology, the Christian life is not an escape mechanism from the realities of life. No, the Christian life does not secure us from the difficulties, pressures and problems that sometimes cause us to be down. In life we will get depressed or down in the dumps, so we will at times sing the blues. We do sometimes feel like God has forgotten us and that we will never get on track again. We all experience the condition that mystics label "the dark night of the soul." (There's nothing wrong with these feelings; just don't allow these feelings to cause you to look in the wrong direction.)

Singer and diva Madonna is one of the wealthiest people in show business and has openly flaunted her self-indulgent lifestyle. A couple of years ago, she was asked in an interview if she was happy. Her response was, "I don't even know anybody who is happy!" Not only was she not happy, but she couldn't think of anyone who was. If you can't be happy when you have it all, how can you be happy?

While looking up statistics about unhappiness in the United States, I discovered these disturbing facts: "Depressive disorders affect approximately 18.8 million American adults or about 9.5% of the U.S. population age 18 and older. Preschoolers are the fastest growing market for antidepressants. At least four percent of preschoolers—over a million —are clinically depressed. The rate of increase of depression among children is an astounding 23 percent."

How can this be, in a land of plenty and prosperity? Could it be that our understanding of what it takes to be happy is distorted? Could it be that our values are warped and have been placed on things that do not bring true joy in life? Is it possible we are walking the wrong path and taking the wrong road? Can it be that we are looking in all the wrong places to make ourselves happy? We still think if we just had enough money, we would be happy. Someone facetiously said, "Those who say that money can't buy happiness don't know where to shop."

In Psalm 42 we see the portrait of an individual who seems to be climbing out of his state of depression and despair. Being down is a normal part of our lives. Like rain, being down is essential for health and life. Though rain is essential, none of us want it to rain all the time. If it is normal to be down, then being down can also be abnormal. Being down becomes abnormal when we allow it to linger on and feed on it.

Though setbacks, discouragement and despair are normal, they must never become the wedge that drives us away from God.

Unlike unbelievers, Christians have a supernatural resource. When an unbeliever gets down, discouraged and in the dumps, he uses devices of escapism such as drugs, alcohol and recreation, only to discover that when he sobers up and his fun is over, he is still down in the dumps. The Christian, however, has divine resources that he can call upon.

When you are feeling down, there are three things you need to do:

1. You need to examine your reason for being down.

Before you can effectively deal with being down, or before you can look upward, it is essential to first examine the cause(s):

- *Absence from the temple of God (v. 1):* The psalmist was far from home, which was Jerusalem. He felt like he was cut off from God, not that he didn't believe in God, but because he was away from the temple where God was worshipped. Thus, he begins this psalm, "As the hart panteth after the water brooks, so panteth my soul after Thee, O God."

- *The taunts of unbelievers (v. 3):* Unbelievers mock you, saying, "If God is dear to you and you to Him, why has He abandoned you? Where is He when you need Him most? Why doesn't He intervene to change your circumstances?"

- *Depression about the memories of better days (v. 4):* "When I remember these things…"

- *The overwhelming trials of life (v. 7):* "Deep calleth unto deep at the noise of thy water-spouts."

The important thing to understand about being down is not that you get out of it, but rather *what* you get out of it. What do you learn from it? If through your despair, if through your discouragement, you keep looking upward, your circumstances will build you up rather than tear you down. If you look upward, eventually the darkness of your depression will become the most fruitful time of your life.

If you know anything about plants, you know that they grow at night rather than in the day. In the day, they receive sunlight, but at night they expand and grow.

2. You need to remind yourself of what you know.

The psalmist tells us how we can win out over this spirit of depression. Notice that he asks himself in the fifth verse, "Why art thou cast down, O my soul?" He does not engage in a pity party; instead, he talks to himself. He reminds himself of what he really knows and finds no reason to be downcast. Contrary to popular opinion, you are not crazy for talking to yourself; it's better to talk to yourself than to allow your depression to talk to you.

The latter portion of this verse says, "For I shall yet praise Him for the help of His countenance." Challenge yourself to do what your spiritual self knows should be done: Put your hope in God. Often we find ourselves in the dungeon of despair. Though our circumstances are beyond logic and reason, I can tell you that God has a strategy for bringing you through victoriously.

3. You need to remember you have hope.

In verse eight, the psalmist says, "Yet the Lord will command His lovingkindness in the daytime and in the night His song shall be with me, and my prayer unto the God of my life." The psalmist was willing to rest his case because his troubles led him to God.

The answer to feeling down is hope. Our hope is not in ourselves, but in God. The hope that we have in God is certain and sure.

Amidst your depression and despair, you can do one of three things. You can endure it, seeking answers through reason or logic, and come up empty. You can escape it, only to discover that when you get where you are going, it will still be there. Or you can learn from it. What will you learn?

- God moves in mysterious ways, His wonders to perform. He plants His footsteps on the sea, and rides upon every storm.

- Judge not the lord by feeble sense, but trust Him for His grace.

- Behind a frowning providence, He hides a smiling face.

- His purpose will ripen fast, unfolding every hour. The bud may have a bitter taste, but sweet will be the flower.

- To cure this spirit of feeling down, cling to Jesus.

The apostle Paul helps us deal with depression by saying, "And we know that all things work together for good to them that love God, to them who are the called according to his purpose" (Rom. 8:28). That's what God does for us. He enables us to say, "No matter how hard it has been, all things work together."

- No matter how threatening the storm clouds may be, all things work together.

- No matter how lonely and friendless I may be, all things work together.

- No matter how saturated by sin you may be, all things work together.

- No matter how painful my past may be, all things work together.

I may not know how He's going to work it out. I just know that some way, somehow, God is working it out.

- Whatever the problem, God is working it out.
- Whatever the perplexity, God is working it out.
- Whatever the roadblock, God is working it out.
- Whatever the depression, God is working it out.
- Whatever the bad news, the good news is that all things work together for good, to them who love God, to them who are called according to his purpose.

The psalmist closes in verse 11 by saying, "For I shall yet praise Him, who is the health of my countenance, and my God."

- If you want to get over this "down" spirit, let your soul look upward.
- Looking downward demands reason and logic, but looking upward demands praise.
- Logic and reason is mind power, but praise is soul power.
- Logic and reason asks, "Why?", but praise says, "Thank you."
- Logic and reason questions God's ability, but praise affirms God's power.
- Logic and reason is debate and dialogue, but praise takes us from hardship to hallelujah.
- Logic and reason is something to talk about, but praise is something to shout about.

Just think and thank. ⌐⊱⊰⌐

Why God's Grace Is So Amazing
(2 Samuel 9:1-13)

⁓C✶Ɔ⁓

REV. DR. A.L. PERKINS SR.

Tabernacle of Faith Missionary Baptist Church
San Francisco, California

So often we hear people talk about God's amazing grace. All through our lives we have been reared on understanding that our God is very gracious. How easy it is to go off what somebody else says, but it becomes more real and meaningful when we are able to experience the grace of God for ourselves.

Everybody who is alive is a grace recipient, whether they choose to admit or deny it. Grace means God's unmerited favor (God giving to me what I don't deserve)—the demonstration of love that is undeserved, unearned and not repayable—or to put in the simplest form, to show kindness. Can you reflect in your mind something you have and didn't deserve, but God was so gracious and still blessed you with it?

We didn't deserve life, but He gave us life. We don't deserve a lot of things, but He still looks beyond our faults and supplies our needs. In this text, I believe we will be able to see how blessed we really are every day and how much God wants to be gracious and bless us.

The backdrop of this text is found in 1 Samuel 18:1, when David and Jonathan made a life covenant or commitment to always look after each other's family, in the event that anything should happen to either of them. Jonathan understood that real early, even though David was not king in Chapter 18. Jonathan died in battle, and he had at least one heir.

When a new person was put in the position of king, normally the new administration would exterminate the past administration. Anything that reminded them of the past they would wipe out so they could have a completely fresh start.

As we look at this text, David is now the king, and he is trying to find anybody from the house of Saul. King David wanted to show kindness to the family of Saul because of Jonathan.

I see a few things in this text that will show us why God's grace is so amazing.

WARRANT—PAST LIFE AND LOCATION

David was willing to show kindness to anyone from Jonathan's family, regardless of Saul being his enemy. His past should have disqualified anyone from Jonathan's family, due to the fact that when a new king took the throne, he normally would wipe out the past administration. God shows us His love in that He has chosen to bless us in spite of our past life.

Not only was David willing to bless Saul's family in spite of his past, but I also see that David was willing to show kindness to Mephibosheth in spite of his present location. David issued a summons for Mephibosheth to come out of Lo-Debar to come and see the king. Lo-debar was a barren, desolate, dry, down and lonely place. It was a place of "no's"—no family, no friends, no future, no joy, no peace, no purpose, no potential and no promise. Lo-Debar was a place of distress, defeat, discouragement, disaster, disappointment, despair and darkness.

Have you ever been to Lo-Debar, or are you still in Lo-Debar? This is one place God does not want us to be. That is why when He calls you out of Lo-Debar, you have to be willing to say good-bye to it. God is calling some of us out, but we want to stay. We keep trying to rationalize in order to see if it's worth staying; but if God is calling you out, it must mean He has something better. But you have to be willing to say good-bye to Lo-Debar. You have to be willing to leave whomever or whatever behind, just like Tom Hanks in the movie *Cast Away* had to make a decision to leave the island and Wilson. You have to say good-bye to Wilson or maybe even give some people the benediction, "The Lord watch between you and me while we're absent, one from another, Amen," because you want to answer God's call to come out of Lo-Debar. If God is calling you to come out, trust that He has a place for you which is better than Lo-Debar. First Peter 2:9 says He has called us out of darkness and into the marvelous light. Come out of Lo-Debar! Some of us don't need to walk but run out of Lo-Debar. If God is calling us to come out of Lo-Debar, we should answer the call to be blessed, because some of us would end up staying and getting real comfortable and complacent if God had not out called us out. Come out of Lo-Debar to be blessed. As Dr. M.T. Thompson says, "God bless us in spite of and not because of."

WORSHIP—IN SPITE OF

My native Texan godfather, Dr. Nathan Johnson, said to me one day, "Learn how to deal with disappointment without being devastated." How often do we allow our present disappointment to not only devastate us but also dictate when and when not to worship God?

In verse six, Mephibosheth, son of Jonathan and the grandson of Saul, came to David, bowed down to the ground and paid homage to him. David said, "Mephibosheth!" "I am your servant," he replied.

We should worship God in spite of our conditions and circumstances. The text says that when Mephibosheth came before David, he immediately bowed down in an act of worship. Worship should not be conditional for any believer; it should not be done out of duty, but desire.

As we look at the present condition of Mephibosheth, we observe that he is crippled—lame in both feet. Like Mephibosheth, we are also crippled. Everybody has something that they are struggling with that slows or hinders their progress. This is why we should be sensitive to each other—because we all are crippled. We all are lamed by our inadequacies, insufficiencies, infirmities, insecurities and iniquities. Lord, help us all to admit and deal with our own condition of lameness. Can we see ourselves in Mephibosheth? Despite his crippled condition, he still worships the king. Can we and do we still worship the king, regardless of our condition? The Lord is still worthy to be worshiped, in spite of whatever we may be facing and will face in life.

Now look at how Mephibosheth responds to King David. He says, "I am the worth of a dead dog." When we worship God, we should always bow in humility to Him because we don't deserve to be in His presence, and at our best, we are filthy rags.

What I believe this passage teaches us is that Mephibosheth refused to complain about the carelessness of someone else. Mephibosheth's lameness was not his fault. When the war was going on and the maid was trying to escape out of the house, she picked up Mephibosheth while running and accidently dropped him, which made him permanently crippled. How many of us have been made crippled because somebody dropped us? How many of us are dealing with lameness due to the negligence of someone else? All of us have hurts caused by somebody else, along with the personal hurts we have caused on our own. But do we ever see Mephibosheth complaining in this text? No. This teaches us not to complain; instead, we need to learn to thank God in spite of our present condition. We all know that complaining won't help. Mephibosheth could have complained because of the carelessness of somebody else. Yet, he recognizes that God allowed his crippled condition, so why should he complain about what God has ordained?

Mephibosheth not only bows once, but he bows again. We should never get tired of bowing to or worshiping God. Truth be told, every time we think of what God has done, we should worship Him. But worship should not always be about what God has done. If you look at Mephibosheth, he worships David for being the king. That's why we should cherish our continual worship of God. When we get to heaven, we will continually worship Him for who He is, not for what He has done. Can you get in the habit of continually worshiping God for being God all by Himself? God is the King of kings and Lord of lords, the Great I Am, the Everlasting Father, Alpha and Omega, the Beginning and the End, God our Everything. As the Psalmist says, "From the rising of the sun until the going down of the same, He is worthy to be praised" (Ps. 113:3).

WARRANTY—INSPIRING

According to verse 11, Mephibosheth has the privilege of no longer being a stranger but a child of King David. King David adopts Mephibosheth into his family. As discussed in Galatians 4:5 and 7, King David does this to show Mephibosheth's worth to him. By his adoption into the family, Mephibosheth is given access to the king at all times. Likewise, we have access today that we may obtain mercy in our time of need. Mephibosheth not only has access to the king; but he also has the assurance that he will always be a part of the family, regardless of his past and even his present mistakes. They do not exempt him from being a part of the family of God. That is why the hymn says, "Blessed assurance, Jesus is mine!/Oh what a foretaste of glory divine/Heir of salvation, purchase of God/Born of His Spirit, washed in His blood!" This should be our story and song, just as it was for Mephobosheth—praising our Savior all the day long.

Mephibosheth is able to have peace because of two reasons. The first is the presence of the king. Whenever you are in the presence of the king, you are in a peaceful position. He who has our King has peace, because He is the Prince of Peace. Also, He brings along with that peace protection, provision and His preserving power. You don't have to fret about your enemies because God will protect you. When you don't know when or where to go, God will provide because He can go ahead of us and see what we cannot see in the "not yet," although we are in the "right now." So, as we walk in faith, we trust that God has gone ahead and worked something out in the "not yet" so that when we get to the "not yet," He can make it the "right now." We are able to give Him thanks and praise because sometimes we know what He has done or who He has moved in order for us to make spiritual progress and grow spiritually in the Word.

Mephibosheth also can have peace because he is now in a place that is totally different from Lo-Debar, the place of no pasture or progress but rather pity and confusion. He is now in Jerusalem, which means "peace." He has peace with the king, which suggests that no matter what you do or where you are, you can have peace because you are at peace with the king. As the hymn "What a Friend We Have in Jesus" says, "Oh, what peace we often forfeit/Oh, what needless pain we bear/All because we do not carry everything to God in prayer."

Mephibosheth now has a permanent promise that will never expire but will remain forever. How good it is to know that the promises of our God will never end! Mephibosheth had the assurance that he would be at the king's table every day. I am quite sure that Mephibosheth is very grateful and appreciative, because in Lo-Debar there was a lack of food, and even in some instances, nothing at all. But now he has plenty, and his cup will be running over because he is in the presence of the king. Thank God that all of His promises are eternal! Truth be told, that is what we are standing on and sustained upon from day to day. You do know what a promise is when Psalm 23 says, "The Lord is my Shepherd; I shall not want."

God has many of these reassuring promises in His Word: "The Lord is my light; whom shall I fear?" (Ps. 27:1). "The grass may wither and the flower may fade, but the word of our God will last forever" (Isa. 40:8). "Weeping may endure for a night, but joy will come in the morning" (Ps. 30:5). "With God all things are possible" (Matt. 19:26). "Seek ye first the kingdom of God and His righteousness and all these things will be added unto you" (Matt. 6:33). "Trust in the Lord with all thine heart and lean not to thy own understanding. In all thy ways acknowledge Him and He shall direct your path" (Prov. 3:5). "My God shall supply all of your needs according to his riches in glory in Christ Jesus" (Phil. 4:19). Thank God for His promises that continue from day to day!

Everybody needs a covering, and how encouraging it is to know that God will provide our covering for us. First, He is gracious to us by giving us a covering because we don't deserve it. Second, He is merciful to provide it because He does not give to us what we do deserve. I define mercy as God not giving to me what I do deserve; I define grace as God giving to me what I don't deserve.

So dinner is about to be served, and everybody is sitting in their respected places at the table. Of course, David is at the head because he is the king. As we look around the table, we see Absalom, of all people, who didn't deserve to be there because he was the son who tried to overthrow his dad's kingdom. You see Tamar, the sister who was raped by her own brother. Little Baby Solomon is in his high chair. Everybody is preparing to say grace and eat when David says, "Wait, all my children are not here. Wait, somebody is missing." Everybody is looking around the table saying, "Who is it?" when all of a sudden, you hear *cha-cha boom, cha-cha boom, cha-cha boom, cha-cha boom, cha-cha boom.* Mephibosheth is coming to the table as a cripple, but he's coming because he knows the king invited him. The king wouldn't have invited him if he didn't have something for him he needed. Everybody is looking at each other and saying, "Why does he get to sit at the table? Who told him he could come to the table?" But Mephibosheth keeps on walking, *cha-cha boom*, till he finally gets to his seat where he finds his place. The first thing he does is scoot all the way up to the table so he can look like everybody else. He knew that when you're at the table, everybody is in on the same level. At the table, you can't tell if anybody is messed up. You can't even see Mephibosheth's lameness because the tablecloth has covered it up. The tablecloth represents God's mercy. Thank God for His mercy! It was gracious to allow him to be included, but mercy then covered him. Likewise, God has promised to give us new mercies every morning so that we may have a covering. Thank God for the tablecloth of mercy that covers us day after day!

So why is God's grace so amazing? Not only did He save Mephibosheth, but He also saved us. I don't know why Jesus loves me;

I don't know why He cares. I don't know why He sacrificed for me. Oh, but I'm glad, I'm glad, I'm glad, He did! I may not be the best at anything nor have the best of everything. Sometimes I feel like I am the least of all. But I know Someone knows everything, and to me He is my everything. I am happy just to know I am His child: His name is Jesus, the righteous son of God. He is the lily of the valley; He's the bright and morning star. His name is Jesus. He's my everything, and I'm happy just to know that I'M HIS CHILD. That is why God's grace is so amazing.

My Best Friend Is My Enemy's Son!
(I Samuel 18:1-12)

❧

DR. ERROL A. REDWELL SR.

Original Mount Pleasant Missionary Baptist Church
Chicago, Illinois

Jonathan was the eldest son of Saul, king of Israel, and David was the youngest son of Jesse, a farmer in Israel. These two young men became the best of friends, but David ended up becoming the enemy of his best friend's father.

David entered the scene here in the text as a victor turned enemy. After the slaying of the Philistine giant Goliath, David—the small, handsome, ruddy-cheeked, little shepherd boy—became the hero of Israel, while at the same time becoming the enemy of the King.

Prior to his demise, Goliath had been in the valley of Elah, terrorizing the army of Israel. Every day when Goliath appeared on the battleground, he called for a man of Israel to come out and fight against him. He promised that if Israel's man defeated him, the army of the Philistines would serve them; but if he defeated Israel's man, then the army of Israel would have to serve them. So, he would come out daily, breathing out threats and slaughter toward Israel in an act to either intimidate them or cause them to fight.

One day, while Goliath was antagonizing and threatening the army of Israel, this little boy, Jesse's youngest son, entered the valley where the battle was arrayed. The archenemy of Israel was calling for a man to fight against him when David showed up and heard him. On this day, David, even though he was only supposed to be checking on the status of the war to share with his father back home, responded to the call of Goliath. David did not intentionally come to the valley to fight the giant who represented the army of the Philistines. David had only come to drop off some supplies for his brothers engaged in the war.

As a matter of fact, David wasn't even of age to fight in this war, or any other war. Based on the legal age of Jewish men fighting or enlisting, David wasn't of age. A man had to be 20 years of age to fight in a war, and at the time David was approximately 18 years of age. But because this war and David's fighting in it was God-ordained, no one ever asked David how old he was. David simply showed up to perform one duty, when he took on an altogether different one. David stepped up to the battlefront and answered the call of the giant. After all, there was no one up to this point who was courageous enough to take this mighty Philistine giant on. It appeared as if they were afraid.

DAVID'S "FIXED" VICTORY

Notice how this battle took the turn from threats and torments to total triumph. First of all, David came to the battleground without any weapons or battle fatigues on at all. He was dressed in his ordinary clothes, only carrying food that his father had sent for his sons who were enlisted in this war. The only other thing that David had on his person (that one wouldn't think would be of any use in a situation such as this) was his slingshot that he often carried. Other than that, David had nothing to do battle with or defeat a man the size of this giant Goliath. David only had a slingshot; however, he didn't even have one stone to put in it.

When David made up his mind to fight the giant, he first stopped by the brook in the valley and gathered some stones to put into his slingshot. One could never imagine a little boy of David's size with such a small weapon in the form of a slingshot defeating a man of Goliath's size. One would have been foolish to think that a slingshot would do any damage or cause any pain to a man that large. However, because this fight was fixed in every way, God, who was David's unseen partner and the weapon of mass destruction, stepped in and fought this fight for Israel by using David.

Strangely enough, when David prepared himself and pulled stones out of the brook, he only chose five, and the five that he selected were smooth stones. I am not certain why these stones were smooth, but I do know that the number five is the number of grace. I also know that there would be no other way David or anyone else for that matter could have or would have defeated a man of Goliath's stature, stamina or strength without God's grace.

David stepped up boldly and courageously without whimpering or weakening, pulled out one of the five stones from his bag, and loaded it into his sling to hurl in the direction of Goliath. With all of his strength, David cast the stone in the air, releasing it into the hands of the One who controls the air, that He might direct it into the face of this mighty terror. And God did just that. God took control of the stone after David released it, and with David's projected targeted area in the mind of God, He caused the stone to land where David had envisioned it landing. David's first and only necessary stone to defeat this giant called Goliath landed in his forehead, knocking him unconscious to the ground. After this, David stepped upon his opponent, removed his foe's weapon and decapitated him, defeating him totally. Israel's enemy was now dead, defeated and done with. David had bested him, and the people were proud of this little boy who minded his father's sheep. David's ability to do what Saul was unable to do, along with the recognition of the people of Israel (especially the women), caused David to become the king's enemy.

Upon David's return from the battle with the giant, he saw and heard the chants, dancing and celebration of his victory by the women of Israel. The women were filled with excitement over what David had just done that no other man in Israel could, including Saul who was their king. They were so moved with joy that they celebrated with a song that they had made up to describe what David had just done in comparison to what Saul had done, relating to both of their war records. They chanted while dancing and playing their musical instruments in the streets of the city, "Saul hath slain his thousands, and David his ten thousands."

When these words were heard by King Saul, he was moved with envy. Saul became jealous of young David for three reasons:

1. *David's victory in slaying Goliath.* Saul never imagined in his wildest dreams that this little shepherd boy would defeat or destroy this tall, towering, tormenting giant.

2. *The emphasis and praise that was placed on David instead of Saul who was the king.* The women, without fear or hesitation, expressed their praises and displayed their excitement about David's victory over their number-one enemy. Hearing the chants that compared David's one-time victory with Saul's numerous victories provoked Saul to take on a posture of rage against David. To Saul, David's victory over Goliath did not merit him any song or celebration of this magnitude, if any at all.

3. *David had done and accomplished something that Saul didn't and had not yet done.* David had killed the enemy of Saul and Israel!! And he did it single-handedly, without a weapon of war—just a slingshot and one stone.

FRIENDSHIP IN THE ENEMY'S HOUSE

Although the King saw David as an enemy because of his envy and jealousy, God was working behind the scenes by giving David a friend in the king's family who would defend David and his honor against the king. Strangely enough, David's best friend and defense against the king's rage was going to be the king's own son, Jonathan.

This friendship began to develop upon David's return from his brief battle, when he was brought before Saul to tell him what actually occurred with his encounter with Goliath and how he defeated him. After David had finished his conversation with the king, there was an unexplained, unexpected and immediate move of the heart and emotions of Jonathan, who had been listening to the story. The text declares that the soul of Jonathan was knit with the soul of David. Jonathan could relate to David because both of them were young men. The king's son extended himself and became united with David, which created strong soul ties between them. Jonathan went further to develop his friendship with David by making a covenant with him to remain friends for as long as they both lived. Their hearts united that day, and they became true friends to the point of being best friends for the remainder of their lives.

The king realized what was taking place in the life of his son Jonathan and the young man that he struggled to accept at this point in his life. He pretended to accept David by inviting him to move in with them and giving him a major military position. David accepted the offer and the position, not realizing that the king had a motive for destroying him. But God had one in the king's house who would be used to alter the negative motives of the king. Jonathan was truly David's best friend, even in the face of his father's rage and fury!!

Even then, Jonathan showed his love and loyalty for his friend by defending him from his father's rage and fits of anger. He did this on several occasions by talking to his father in David's defense and getting David out of the way of his father's anger whenever Saul would seek to bring harm to him. Saul often erupted into fits of anger and even tried to kill David twice by throwing javelins at him. However, each time Saul made an attempt on his life, David escaped his wrath because of Jonathan, who either warned him or spoke up in his defense. Jonathan even tried to tone down Saul's ill will toward David by showing his father the good in David, as well as the good in what he had done by defeating the Philistines. Finally, he tried to get his father to realize how he would bring harm to himself if he killed David, because then he would be shedding innocent blood.

God moved upon the heart of Jonathan, causing him to act as a drum major for peace between his father and his best friend, who was his father's enemy. There was no way that Jonathan and David's friendship would have lasted in the face of what was going on between David and Saul, unless their friendship had been ordained of God. Their friendship went against normal human rules. There was no way Jonathan was supposed to love or be friends with anyone that his father disliked, didn't approve of, or was at odds with—like he was with David.

However, what we need to understand about friends and friendship is the fact that,

- True friends are hard to find.
- When you have a true friend, you not only have a rare commodity, but a jewel.
- Ultimately, we must realize that true friendships cannot be destroyed based upon blood relations or anything else because "what God joins together, no man can put asunder."

In conclusion, David is a witness that God will raise up a friend for us, even in our enemy's family, who will love us loyally and unconditionally.

When Vipers Strike
(Acts 28:1-6)

BISHOP KEITH W. REED SR.

Sharon Baptist Church
Philadelphia, Pennsylvania

The great apostle called Paul was the one whom God had saved miraculously on the road to Damascus. It was there that Paul, formerly known as Saul of Tarsus, had an encounter of the third kind. He met the Head of the church after being a persecutor of the Lord's body. You remember Saul of Tarsus. He wreaked havoc in the Christian community. He was not prejudiced: He would arrest and abuse men, women and children. Anyone who named the name of Christ and was of that movement called the Way, Saul sought to get out of the way. It was that Saul whom Jesus knocked to the ground with the light. After a brief dialogue and discussion, even Saul of Tarsus found that his arms were too short to box with God. As a result of that encounter, he became a child of God.

That same Saul who was converted into Paul and persecuted the Church was now being persecuted by the Church. God used him to help his friend and confidante Barnabas as they teamed up to do ministry until the break and fracture in the fellowship. Then it was Silas and Timothy, and others came along after that. We look at his life as it began to unfold in the Book of Acts. One passion that Paul always had was that he wanted to go to Rome and preach the gospel. He probably thought he was going to get to Rome by the way of a cruise ship, but instead he got a hitch as a prisoner. He was a prisoner for preaching; he was a prisoner for the cause of Christ. Here he was, preaching the gospel and getting arrested, literally lied upon and maligned. He was virtually denied his rights until he appealed to Caesar.

So here he was on this ship, and as they started going toward Rome, Acts 27:21 said that Paul got a revelation. An angelic visitor had come to him and said, "Tell the captain and the owner of the ship that they ought not to sail now because they're going to run into some turbulent storms." He went, as a prisoner, and shared with them that they needed to wait because this was not a good time to sail. Paul said, "I just need to let you know I had a visitor last night, and I was told to tell you not to sail." The captain of the ship and the owner said to Paul, for the lack of a better term, "Sit down. You're nothing but a prisoner who's supposed to be a preacher. We are sailors; we know the seas. We have this under control."

They proceeded to head toward Rome; and when they first started out, it was pleasant. It looked like it was going to be a good sail. But suddenly out of the clear blue sky—the sky was bright, the sun was blazing—the wind started blowing. The waves started dashing. As the ship began to spin and toss, they thought at first that it was just a normal storm. But several days had passed, and the sun still seemed to be eclipsed. It looked like perpetual night, with daylight nowhere in sight. The winds continued to blow, and the waves continued to dash. Then, all of a sudden, Paul made his way to the captain and the owner of the ship and said, "I told you that God said you ought not to sail now. But I've got another word for you. If you stay with the ship, you will not lose a soul. The vessel might be broken, and we may lose cargo; but if you stay with the ship, not a soul will not be lost." The Bible said they continued to sail through the storm. They were literally exhausted because they were trying to manage, despite the storm.

It was the apostle Paul who took leadership in the midst of the storm and said to those who were on the ship, "Calm down. Get something to eat because you're weary. You need strength to make it through the storm." He then blessed the bread, and they began to eat. But then, all of a sudden, the ship ran aground against the rocks. It began to crumble and break into pieces, so they began to jump ship. It was the apostle Paul who said, "Grab a hold of a piece of the vessel." Acts 27: 44 said that they made it to shore on broken pieces. (Sometimes when life does break down, stay with what you know. Stay with who you know because the God whom we serve is able to bring you in on broken pieces.) The Bible says that "when they arrived to an island they did not know until after they got there, they had escaped the storm." Then they knew that the island they were on was called Malta.

SEASONS FOR TESTING AND RESTING

Verse two of the 28th chapter says that when they got there, the "natives treated them with unusual kindness." There are a couple of principles here that we need not pass by without mentioning them. The first is that we will not avoid storms. Storms can come at any time, but if we do what we know and stick with who we know, God is able to bring us through storms. Don't ever think that because you know God and have been pardoned for your sin; because you read your Bible and have your devotionals; because you pray, tithe and give your offering; because you're committed and loyal to the fellowship and to its Head, Jesus the Christ; because you have friends and family; and you are a witness or testifier of the goodness of our Savior, it exempts you from storms.

We have to go through storms because they do a few things for us. First of all, storms have a way of showing us what we are not. They have a way of letting us know that we are not what we think we are. We don't know anything until we're tested. We have to go through storms for us to be validated in what we do know. The other thing about storms is that they not only show us what we don't know, what we're made of and what we're not; but they also show us who He is. Storms show us what He's capable of doing, and they have a way of imparting character in our lives. They make us toughen up and cause us to realize that God is able to keep those promises to us which He has made. Even though we walk through the valley of the shadow of death, yet we ought not to fear any evil because He is with us. His rod and staff will comfort us.

But the other thing we can learn about storms through this passage is this: *After every storm or period of testing, there is always a season of resting.* God does not allow us to constantly go through storms, because He knows our frame. He knows what we are made of and what we can take. He knows what we can handle. He knows that when it gets too hard, He has to stop it so we can have a season of rest. In 1 Corinthians 10:13, Paul says that "there is no temptation overtaken us that is not common to man. But God is faithful, and He will give us a door of escape that we might be able to bear it." There are some trials you and I can handle, but even they have a stopwatch on them. God knows when to stop and when to start. God knows how heavy the testing can be and how far it can go. God knows when, where and how. When God says it is enough, it will be enough because He knows we can only take so much. *Because after every period of testing, there is always a season of resting.*

Even our Lord, after being baptized in the third chapter of Matthew, was driven into the wilderness in the fourth chapter by the Spirit to be tempted of the Devil. The Bible says that right after the last temptation, the Devil left him for a season. Then the Bible says that angels came down to minister to him. *Because after every major period of testing, there is always a season of resting.*

The question is: What season are you in? If you are in the season of testing, fret not, for our God is with you. He is up to something. He is allowing it because He knows you're able to handle it. He knows what you can bear. Psalm 139:1 says that "He knows [your] rising and [your] sitting down." He knows your frame, for "He has searched [you] and known [you]." He knows the way you take. As Job said, "Though He slay me, yet will I trust Him" (Job 13:15). I've learned to wait until my change comes. Yes, God knows! *After your season of testing, He will always bring a season of resting.*

BUT WHEN...

The text says that the natives treated them with unusual kindness. They began to gather sticks and wood to kindle a fire, and it made the passengers feel welcome because of the rain that was falling and the cold. That makes sense, after coming through a storm like that—after being shipwrecked and having to jump into the water and holding on to broken pieces, just to make it to dry land. They were cold because of the rain and the storm. The Bible says, "But when Paul began to gather the bundle of sticks and laid them on the fire, a viper came out because of the heat."

The New King James Version says, "But when Paul...", which refers to verse two of Chapter 28. For it says, "The natives were gathering sticks for the fire." The natives of that island called Malta were doing what needed to be done. When they gathered the sticks and put them together to kindle a fire, nothing happened. But verse three says, "But when Paul..." It's strange to me that when others do a deed, nothing seems to happen. The truth is, however, that the viper was there all the time.

There's a principle here: It's all right to let other people do some things for others; but when you, a child of God, do something that's going to make a significant impact on someone else's life, you'll find out that you will be a victim of circumstances. Put your name there after "But when…" Things will happen when you do it, because it's going to be significant. When you do it, there's going to be an anointing on it. When you do it, God is going to be glorified. When you do it, the Savior will be exalted. When you do it, lives are going to be changed. Everybody else can do it, but when Paul had gathered the bundle of sticks and laid them on the fire, the Bible says a viper came out.

When you see other organizations do stuff, they just press on and do it. There seems to be no contention, no rebuttal or no opposition. But when the Church of Jesus Christ seeks to do something, isn't it strange how certain people come out of the woodwork? People that you've never known before and organizations you never knew existed rally themselves against that which is right and righteous. Isn't it strange? Have you noticed that during the ministry of our Savior opposing parties existed during His tenure that hated one another? The Pharisees did not like the Sadducees. The Herodians did not like the other groups. They all had something against each other. But when Jesus came along, it seemed that He was the common denominator. All of a sudden, those who had opposed each other became allies. They began to team up with one another to come against the One who was doing ministry more effectively than they were doing it. When Jesus came along, no one had ever heard it like He said it. Nobody had ever seen it like He did it—so much so that people began to wonder, "What manner of man is this? How does such a man speak with such authority?" (Luke 4:32). Rabbi So-and-So or Scribe So-and-So would teach some lesson from the Torah, but they would always be quoting someone else. But Jesus came along and said, "You have heard it said...but I say unto you..." (Matt. 5:21), and He would go on and say something that was contrary to what was already said. Those who were working against each other had now found a common denominator. Don't ever think that if you're going to do anything for the King and the kingdom, those opposing parties won't come out of the woodwork. The Bible says, "But when Paul gathered the sticks and laid the bundle on the fire, all of a sudden a viper appeared."

VIPERS: LAYING LOW, LAUNCHING OUT AND LATCHING ON

The first thing that this passage tells us about vipers is that they lay low. They are always there. That viper did not show up when Paul showed up; that viper was already there. That viper was there near a bundle of sticks; but as long as it was cold, that viper laid low. As long as its atmosphere or central area of contact was not affected, that viper laid low. As long as no one came and kicked up a disturbance around that viper and the atmosphere surrounding it remained cold, it laid low. As long as you don't do anything with them or bother them, they won't bother you. They will lay low.

There are huge differences between snakes and sheep. Vipers are cold-blooded animals; their skin and scales are cold to the touch. But if you touch sheep, they will be warm. As long as the atmosphere is cold and as long as there is no disturbance, vipers will lay low. On the other hand, you can't be sheep and not have heat. If you're a snake, you're going to stay cold; but if you're a sheep, you'll bring heat. In this story, the more sticks the natives put on the fire, the warmer it became. The warmer it became, the more it changed the climate of where the viper was because it was lay- ing low. When the climate changes because of the heat and the circum- stances around the viper, it disturbs its body temperature so it can't lay low. The next thing it's going to do is launch out from the fire.

Don't ever think you're going to be around a viper person with all your Holy Ghost heat without moving around and raising your hands. Because of this spiritual heat, you've got to say, "Hallelujah!" Because of the heat, you've got to move. You can't sit and lay low and be cold and indifferent. You've got to jump up and say, "Amen!" You've got to say and do something. You've got to give praise and worship, which causes heat. What happens is this: As long as nothing is done, you'll never know there's a viper around you. But when you do something other than what the viper is known for doing, you really disturb them and show them up for what they really are. That's why they've got to move from laying low to launching out. "How dare you talk about praise? And I have not opened my mouth." "How dare you show me up by testifying how good He is? And I have been testifying all these years." "How dare you get excited beyond the music and beyond a song?" "How dare you have a Pentecostal experience because of some words out of a book? And I've been sitting around under that book for years, and it hasn't moved me yet."

Vipers launch out because you've disturbed their atmosphere, and they get mad. You can tell they're vipers. You don't have to be a rocket scientist or deep in the Spirit. You don't have to have revelations or illuminations on situations. You can spot a viper a mile off. The minute you cause a disturbance where they used to be comfortable, now you're making them feel uncomfortable. When you're praising, shouting and raising your hands in response to the unction of the Holy Spirit and the truth of God's Word, you can spot that viper. When you're saying, "Amen!" and "Hallelujah!," you don't cut your step around a viper who looks at you and says, "You're not all that!" They don't know what it takes because they don't have what it takes: That's why they're cold and indifferent. You show them something different by your heat, so they are not going to lay low. They're going to launch out.

Not only do vipers lay low and launch out, but vipers also latch on. The Bible says that when Paul caused a disturbance in the atmosphere, the viper moved. When the viper launched out, it latched onto his hand. Any time you provoke a viper to move from its cold, indifferent posture, when it launches out, it is accurate. It's going to latch on. You need to know that if you are a sheep and find yourself around a bunch of snakes; but you don't know that they're snakes, they are still snakes. They hiss on everything. You can tell snakes because they hiss on what the choir sings. They hiss on where the ushers seat people. They hiss on the worship experience. They hiss on the Word of God. They hiss about the teaching. They hiss about the preaching. They hiss about the order. They hiss about the climate changing. They hiss about the praise. They hiss about worship. They hiss about giving glory. They hiss about giving. They hiss about everything, because vipers are hissed off. They keep on hissing about everything. And they want to turn your baaing into hissing by latching onto you. They try to fill you with what they are. When they try to fill you with their venom, they'll try to snatch your praise. They'll poison your worship. They'll poison your joy and peace because they've latched on, and they want to fill you with what they are. And they're nothing more than filled with poison. They really are trying to conform you into professional hissers.

You will be bit. I'm trying to find ways to soften this reality for you, but the text did say that the viper latched on. As a child of God, your temperature will change the atmosphere. When you're sitting next to a viper, you will be bit. I'm sorry that I can't give you better news, but I can tell you that if you move in a certain way, it won't latch on. You will be bit, but you don't have to be affected by the bite. The Bible said that when the viper struck at Paul—when the viper moved from laying low to launching out, when the viper latched on—those around him felt that he was going to die because they said, "Truly, this man is a murderer." They began to surmise and assume that if Paul was doing what he was supposed to be doing, he wouldn't have gotten bit. This proves the point that you can be doing what you're supposed to do, and you can be saying what you're supposed to be saying; but that doesn't mean you will be exempt from being bit. There are bad things that happen to good people.

When the viper latched on, the Bible said that the viper injected its venom. But the good news is that viper didn't know who he was biting. He didn't know what kind of person Paul was. That viper didn't know that Paul had some antivenom in him that was running through his blood. When that viper bit Paul, the antivenom kicked in, and it said something like this: "No weapon or warfare will be able to prosper that comes up against you" (Isa. 54:17). The viper is trying to turn him into what it is, but the antivenom serum kicks in: "If any man be in Christ, he is a new creature. All things are passed away, behold all things have become new" (2 Cor. 5:17). The antivenom serum kicked in because the venom tried to fill him with fear: "The Lord is my light and my salvation; whom shall I fear?" and "The Lord is the strength of my life; of whom shall I be afraid?" (Ps. 27:1).

I'm glad that within my being I have antivenom serum, so when vipers bite it kicks in: "Weeping may endure for a night, but joy will come in the morning" (Ps. 30:5). We have antivenom running through our veins because the Holy Spirit keeps pumping it in so the Enemy won't win: "Put on the whole armor of God that you may be able to stand against the wiles of the Devil. Make sure you have on the helmet of salvation. Make sure you put on the breastplate of righteousness. Make sure your feet are shod with the preparation of the gospel of peace. Make sure you take up the Sword of the Spirit, which is the word of God" (Eph. 6: 14-17). Whenever the viper bites, you strike back. Stand firm! Stand strong, because God isn't through with you yet.

Defilement Behind
the Cosmetics of the Temple
(Ezekiel 8:1-18)

꧁❀꧂

PASTOR BUCAS STERLING III

Kettering Baptist Church
Upper Marlboro, Maryland

A few weeks ago, between my first and second worship services, I came across a young child in the administrative office of the church. There she was, as cute as a button, putting on lip gloss. Not just any lip gloss—it was pink, glitter-enhanced, cherry-flavored lip gloss. I thought to myself, "This is unusual for such a young child to be decorating her tender, young, pink lips already." Therefore, I inquired how old she was. She aptly responded with enthusiasm, "I'm three years old." I thought to myself, "Wow! At three, this child has already been introduced to cosmetics."

Cosmetics are typically used to enhance, complement and—in some cases—hide unsightly appearances. In the United States, we spend billions of dollars a year on cosmetics from Maybelline, Mary Kay, MAC and many others. In 2006, over 14 billion dollars were spent on cosmetic surgery for anything from lips, bottoms and boobs to injections and extractions. It seems that we are consumed with covering and altering our appearances.

Regardless of what we do to hide behind cosmetics, God always knows what lies underneath the surface. In this powerful yet sad passage of Ezekiel, we witness God snatching Ezekiel up by the hair, out of his dwelling place in exile filled with the elders of Israel, and transporting him supernaturally some 500 miles back to Jerusalem so that He may show him the defilement behind the cosmetics of the temple. Described in 1 Kings 6, the outer walls of this temple were built with quarried stones, but the interior was comprised of cedar beams, cedar panels, cedar ornaments, beveled framed windows and cypress floors—all overlaid with pure gold. There was an outer court, an inner court, an outer sanctuary (the holy place) and an inner sanctuary (the Holy of Holies) containing the Ark of the Covenant, where the presence of God dwelled. Aesthetically, the beauty of the temple remains unmatched by any other building in history. Yet, as is the case with many temples, behind its cosmetics the defilement ran deep, which displeased God.

FRONT-DOOR DISTRACTIONS:
PROVOKING GOD TO JEALOUSY

In verses one through six, Ezekiel's journey revealed that the defilement behind the cosmetics of the temple began with front-door distractions. At the front of the temple, with its quarried stones, cedar beams, cedar panels, cedar ornaments, beveled framed windows and cypress floors, (all overlaid with pure gold), was positioned a guardian goddess of the gate, referred to as "the image of jealousy." This goddess, perhaps Asherah, was positioned in such a way at the temple entrance that it provided an immediate distraction to the devoted loyalty to Jehovah that the worshippers were instructed by the Law to have.

As a front-door distraction, this goddess served to provoke God to jealousy—defined as a natural response consisting of apprehension and protection of a loved one or thing. As it relates to God, jealousy is the fuel for fury resulting from an individual's lack of full devotion to Him alone, which He requires. In some ways the front-door distraction begins to divert God's demonstration of love as His jealousy, anger and fury are provoked.

A very good question for self-examination would be to ask yourself, "What is at the front door of my temple that is distracting me from my sole devoted worship of God, thus provoking Him to jealousy?" Perhaps for you it may be a title, a position of power, a denomination or a building.

DARK-ROOM WORSHIP:
PAYING HOMAGE TO IDOLS IN PRIVATE

Defilement behind the cosmetics of the temple begins with front-door distractions but goes even deeper with dark-room worship (vv. 7-13). Dark-room worship happens in very private places or ways so it will not be discovered. Ezekiel traveled to what reminds me of a 1940s gangsters' hideout—a peephole in the wall. Seventy elders would dig through the wall, go past the door on the other side and enter a chambered section in the temple. There, in the dark, they worshipped gods of their previous bondage drawn on the wall in separate private chambers.

The elders worshipped in God's temple with its quarried stones, cedar beams, cedar panels, cedar ornaments, beveled framed windows and cypress floors overlaid with pure gold. All the while, they worshipped foreign gods in private, rationalizing that God did not see them, having forsaken the land.

What god of your past do you worship in the dark when you believe God does not see you? Psalm 139 reminds us that there is no place we can go to escape His presence.

Dark-room worship is practiced by a variety of people. As we see from this text, while looking behind the cosmetics of the temple we will often discover that some of those involved may surprise us. Jaazaniah, for example, was found in the temple leading the elders in dark-room worship even though his family had a history of faithful devotion to God. Past family history does not prevent people from engaging in dark-room worship. If God allowed us behind the cosmetics of today's temple, we too may find some unexpected people participating in dark-room worship.

NORTH-GATE WEEPERS:
LAMENTING OVER WHAT IS DEAD

The Lord encouraged Ezekiel to turn again, because behind the cosmetics of the temple, defilement began with front-door distractions, regressed further with dark-room worship and became even worse with north-gate weepers (v. 14).

Much to the astonishment of Ezekiel, a group of women at the entrance of the north gate was weeping for the god Tammuz. This god was known to be dead, yet they were defiling the temple of the living God with its quarried stones, cedar beams, cedar panels, cedar ornaments, beveled framed windows and cypress floors (all overlaid with pure gold) by wailing for the resurrection of Tammuz—a god who could not save, who could not deliver and who himself was in need of their help.

Interestingly enough, even today behind the cosmetics of God's house we can find people still weeping over that which is dead. At times it may involve a previous pastor who has gone home to be with the Lord, an old program that died many years ago or perhaps even an old way or place of worship that no longer exists. The danger is that we may find ourselves worshipping that which was never intended to be worshipped and only defiles God's house.

INNER-COURT IDOLATERS: DISRESPECTING GOD

The final movement in Ezekiel's visit behind the cosmetics of the temple was prompted by God saying to him, "...turn again, you will see greater abominations than these." Though defilement behind the cosmetics of the temple began with front-door distractions, regressed further with dark-room worship and became even worse with north gate weepers, it culminated with inner-court idolaters (vv. 16–18).

In the inner court of God's temple cosmetically arrayed with quarried stones, cedar beams, cedar panels, cedar ornaments, beveled framed windows and cypress floors (all overlaid with pure gold), 25 men were bowing to the sun, all the while showing their utmost disrespect for God by turning their backs and backsides on Him. They openly disrespected the very God who delivered them, established them and provided for them by choosing to worship His creation above Him in His temple.

Their blatant disrespect for God only earned them the accusation of filling the land with violence. In other words, they had taught the rest of the land to maintain the cosmetics of the temple, but behind the walls they visibly portrayed a different message—that it was all right to turn your back and even your backside to God. To give us a clearer picture of what God felt about their behavior, the term in the original text can be better translated, "They run the branch up My nose." This phrase is one used to demonstrate a blatantly obscene gesture, for which God declared that He would act in fury and refuse to hear their cries. In what ways today are we performing inner-court idolatry and running the branch up God's nose? How often are we worshipping His creation above Him?

WHAT DEFILES OUR TEMPLE?

A review of this passage may lead us to be hard and judgmental toward Israel. Before we do that, however, remember that 1 Corinthians 3:16 says "you are the temple...", and 1 Peter says that, instead of being quarried stones, we are "living stones." Now, this passage becomes personal as we search ourselves to determine what defilements may be behind our cosmetics. Are we guilty of front-door distractions, dark-room worship, north-gate weeping or inner-court idolatry? In our cosmetics of living stones, beams, panels, windows and floors (all overlaid with His blood), is there defilement that will provoke God to jealousy or run the branch up His nose?

A defiled temple behind the cosmetics that you and I possess leave us with no sense of hope. Matthew 12:6 reminds us that there came One greater than the temple whom we always found in the temple. On one occasion Jesus cleansed the temple and declared that "if you destroy this temple I will raise it again in three days." Since He always had done exactly what He said He would do, in three days He got up from the grave with all power in His hands. He now has power over death, hell and sin. Therefore, whether we are defiled with front-door distractions, dark-room worship, north-gate weeping or inner-court idolatry, we have a Savior who is able to cover us with His precious blood, cleanse us from all unrighteousness and declare us righteous so that He may dwell in us. ᏤᎾ

What a Difference Jesus Can Make
(Luke 7:11-17)

༄ྂཉ

REV. DR. AL B. SUTTON JR.

Sixth Avenue Baptist Church
Birmingham, Alabama

Life is rarely without painful pictures. Sometimes these scenes and experiences have a way of getting to our hearts, especially the pictures of disadvantaged children in Third World countries who have bloated stomachs and emaciated faces and are struggling daily with insufficient food, dirty water and the absence of health care. Their future seems dark and uncertain.

People are currently being ravaged by tuberculosis in Cairo, and children are being orphaned by the AIDS pandemic in Uganda. Irene, 14, and Nicholas,16, for example, both have lost their parents due to AIDS. Now they have been given the responsibility of being parents to their siblings: providing for and protecting them, working long hours and seeing their own dreams deferred. They realize that they will probably never have an opportunity to get an education since this has now become their new lot in life.

I thought about this just a few years ago while visiting Monrovia Liberia and seeing the smiling faces of 92 orphan kids whose lives have been ruined by civil war. Here they are, now living in abandoned buildings and eating food out of filthy utensils. Here they are, with only one change of clothes, and this seems to be their lot. But I shall never forget that Thursday afternoon when my wife and I sat in that abandoned building during a thunderstorm, listening to those same children singing about the goodness of the Lord while the rain was tapping on that tin roof. If I can borrow a phrase from Diane Sawyer, it was the most spiritually transcendent moment of my life. It is amazing, isn't it, how life sends us those painful pictures? There are certain experiences and scenes that get to your heart, but one of the ways of discerning just how affected you are is determined by what you do as a result of them.

WHY IS JESUS MOVED WITH COMPASSION?

In our text, Jesus had such an experience when He observed that funeral procession coming out of the city gates of Nain while visiting there with His disciples. The city of Nain sits between Endor and Shunem, about 20 miles from Jerusalem and six miles from Nazareth. This is around the area where the prophet Elisha is said to have raised the Shunammite woman's son who had been seized by death.

This young man was being carried out to be buried in the local cemetery outside the city gates. His life had been cut short. Jesus observed the tender scene of this mother going out to bury her one and only son. She had already said good-bye to her husband, and now life was forcing her to say good-bye to her only son. Here was this long funeral procession with the flute and cymbals players and the professional mourners. Friends from the city were seeking to offer solace or comfort to this mother in her hour of loss. When Jesus saw this, He was moved.

I wonder why Jesus was moved. Was it because He had never been to a funeral before? Or could it be that He is moved by every funeral that He sees? Was He moved by the fact that this young man had been cut off in the prime of life before his dreams had been fulfilled?

The truth of the matter is that life is never without limitations, boundaries or time restraints. All of us are living on borrowed time; all our days are numbered. When we come to the realization of that, we learn to deal differently with our lives and relationships. We learn to deal more respectfully with our time, not wasting it. We decide to take advantage of the opportunities that are provided for us because we now understand that when they are gone, they are gone.

Perhaps Jesus grieved when He saw this young man being carried out. He could have grieved because of the sorrow that had overwhelmed this mother; this mother was going to bury her only begotten son in the local cemetery outside the city gates.

The reality is that life is never without suffering. Virgil, the Roman poet, said that it is the nature of things that we live in a world with broken hearts. I seem to understand this reality better as my life continues to move onward. The older I get, the more I understand what F. L. Eliand, the hymnwriter, meant: "Life is filled with swift transitions/Naught of earth unmoved can stand/Build your hopes on things eternal/Hold to God's unchanging hand."

Jesus could have been moved just seeing this mother grieving over her one and only son being buried in the local cemetery. He could have grieved when He saw this procession with the flute and cymbals players, the professional mourners and the friends from the city coming to offer comfort and solace to this mother in her hour of grief. Watching the procession could have moved Him. He had already been moved when He saw Martha and Mary grieving over the passing of Lazarus in the company of their friends and persons from the city of Jerusalem who had come to be with them.

Jesus grieved with these people. Perhaps He grieved seeing that procession, or it may have been that this procession passing by Him was symptomatic of an even greater problem which went all the way back to the first sin of Adam and Eve. Since the fall, the wages of sin has been death. Humanity has been caught in this long, unbroken procession to the grave—from Genesis to Malachi.

JESUS STOPS THE PROCESSION TO THE GRAVE

H.G. Wells, a British fiction author, has written such notable works as *The Island of Dr. Moreau*, *The War of the Worlds*, *The Invisible Man* and *The Time Machine*. He passed away on August 13, 1946. What is interesting is the fact that journalists from all over the world gathered around his deathbed to capture his final words. When he saw the room crowded with these newsmen, the practical joker in him came out. He sat up and said, "Leave me alone! Can't you see I am busy dying?"

What H.G. Wells said in jest is, in a very real sense, what has happened to humanity. Humanity has been about the business of dying. But what if humanity was about the business of living? Jesus wants to stop this long procession to the grave. He wants us to understand that He has come to give us something better. He said, "I came that you might have life and have it more abundantly" (John 10:10). That is why Jesus has stopped this long procession to the grave. That's what Calvary was about: stopping that long procession to the grave by rerouting it. We now can bypass the grave and move into everlasting life.

Seeing this mother going to bury her only begotten son in the local cemetery outside the city gates filled Jesus' heart with compassion. His compassion suggests the motivation behind His miracles; the reason that He intercedes, interrupts and does what He does is because He is moved by compassion. Often He just acts out of compassion.

Once, when Jesus saw a big crowd gathering, He was moved with compassion because they looked like sheep without a shepherd (Mark 6:34). And what about that famous miracle which happened on the back side of a mountain? In this rather barren place, this company of people had been with Jesus three days. He was so moved with compassion that He told His disciples to feed the crowd. They were unable to do so, but He didn't want to send them home unfed because they might have collapsed along the way. So he took a lad's lunch, multiplied it and satisfied the appetite of the multitude. I like the way that Harry Wright phrases it: "Jesus fed them on a few sardines and a handful of crackers." It's amazing what Jesus could do with a little bit: He was able to satisfy the hungry appetites of thousands of men, not including wives and children.

The motivation was compassion. Here, Jesus had compassion on a grieving mother. In the Greek language, this is one of the strongest words that one can possibly use to express sympathy or pity. It speaks of being touched in the deeper places of one's heart. Jesus was truly moved with compassion when He saw this mother going to bury her only son.

It is interesting that the Stoics had problems with this. The Stoics did not see God as sensitive; instead, they believed that God was apathetic, indifferent and insensitive. They thought that God had to be insensitive and indifferent because He had to be in control. In other words, if God was moved by someone else's pain for just a brief period, the control would be in the hands of another. If that was the case, then how did they explain Jesus' tears outside the tomb of Lazarus because of his friend's death or His compassion on a mother who went to bury her only son?

If this is what you think, you need to readjust your theology because the fact is that Jesus came to earth to help us understand that our God is sensitive to our hurts, our pain and our suffering. Our tears are His tears, and our pains are His pains. He is sympathetic to our hurts. I am glad that my God can empathize with me: My God is a priest who can be touched by my infirmities.

JESUS' WORDS MAKE A DIFFERENCE!

The text not only suggests that Jesus is compassionate, but it also says He sought to comfort her. He went up to this mother and said, "Don't weep." Now, if she didn't already know who He was, she probably took those words and threw them in a pot with the myriad responses that she had gotten from different people throughout the day who had sought to comfort her and encourage her in her hour of loss. What she didn't understand was that these weren't some empty, flimsy words thrown from the lips of the Master. (The words of Jesus are different from the words of anybody else. What Jesus offers is what nobody else can offer. These aren't just mere words; this is true comfort because only Jesus can make a difference.)

When Jesus says "Don't cry," He also knows how to dry your tears. He knows how to match the words with the deeds of comfort. When He says to a man who cannot speak, "Speak!", He also looses his stammering tongue. He speaks to the man who cannot hear, but He also opens his deaf ears. To the crippled who cannot stand, He does not simply say stand; but He also gives them the ability to stand on their own feet. He doesn't just say "Quiet!", but he also stills the storm on the Sea of Galilee.

I don't know your predicament or your circumstances, but this is what I know. When you start talking about the living word of Jesus, what you are saying is simply this: God doesn't just speak words; He also knows how to deliver them. He doesn't just speak comfort; He can also bring comfort. He doesn't just speak peace; He can also bring peace. He doesn't just speak hope; He can also bring hope. He doesn't just speak life; He can also bring life. Whatever He speaks, He can also bring to pass.

Jesus sought to comfort this mother. He went from the mother over to the bier on which the corpse was lying. He touched the coffin, and immediately the procession stopped. That seemed to be the rationale for touching it; it was His way of saying that there would be no more need to go that way. After stopping the procession, Jesus said to the young man lying on the pallet, "Young man, I say to you, arise."

Now, if you have looked at the resumé of Jesus, you know that He said this before. When Jairus' daughter passed away, people were crying and wailing. Jesus asked them what the commotion was all about. He told them that the little girl was not dead; she was just sleeping. They laughed at Him, so He put them out. (Sometimes you have got to put folks out if they are not where you are. If they can't see what you see, you can't spend all of your time trying to convince them.) After Jesus puts them out, He takes the mother and father, along with three of His disciples (Peter, James and John) into the room where the little girl is lying on the bed. He says to her, "Little girl, I say arise." It is the "I say" that you must notice because this suggests that the authority abides in Jesus. Why? Because this is the very same voice that spoke in Genesis 1:3, 6, 9, 11, 14 and 20, "Let there be…" This is the voice spoken about in John 1:1: "And the word became flesh, and we beheld Him as the only begotten of the Father, full of grace and truth." This is the creative power of God; what He says is so.

Jesus said, "Young man, I say arise. Do you know who this is? I say the mountains know Me, the valleys know Me and the rivers know Me. Do you know Me? I say arise." And the text says that he sat up. This is an almost direct comparison to the prophet Elijah bending over the son of the widow of Zarephath (1 Kings 17:21) or the prophet Elisha bending over the son of a Shunammite woman (2 Kings 4:34) and bringing them back to life. That is what happens in this text when the young son of the Nain widow sits up: He is complete, whole and healed. He has been resuscitated. Then he speaks, (in contrast to the son of the Shunammite woman, who sneezes seven times as an indication of his recovery.) Then Jesus gives him back to his mother.

Death steals from families, taking children from parents and parents from children and siblings from their brothers and sisters. That's what death does: It robs us of the people we love. Yet, even though death steals, God is able to give back. God is able to reunite people, and so there is this picture of restoration and reunion. I love that Jesus gives him back to his mother.

It is almost a repeat of what happens when the prophet Elijah goes up and resuscitates the son of the widow of Zarephath. He scoops him up in his arms, flies down those stairs and gives him back to his mother, saying, "Look, he is alive!" Then the mother says, "Now I know that you are a prophet. Now I know that you are a man of God and the word of God in your lips is truth" (v. 24). This is the validation of Elijah's prophetic identity.

YOU OUGHT TO PRAISE HIM!

Similarly, this healing miracle appears to validate the prophetic identity of Jesus Christ. When the crowd saw it, they began praising God: "A great prophet is among us; a prophet is risen up among us" (v.

16). When the crowd saw the miracle, they were seized with fear and amazement. They were captured by wonder and began praising God. I think that today the Church is struggling because it has lost its sense of wonder, as though it has not been looking at the miracles of God, the wondrous deeds of God and the extraordinary things of God.

God still visits His people today and stops funeral processions by offering life. Yet this visitation of God often seems to go unnoticed or rejected. When you have been in the presence of God and experienced His miracles and wonders, you ought to praise Him. I still think of that time Peter toiled all night fishing but caught nothing. But then he heard Jesus saying, "Launch out into the deep and let down your net." When he went back out into the water and let down his net, the text said he caught more fish than he was able to haul into the boat. Then, he bowed down at the feet of Jesus right there on the boat and began to worship Him, saying, "Depart from me, for I am a sinful man" (Luke 5:3-8).

I also thought about that anonymous woman of questionable reputation, out of whom Jesus cast seven demons. The Bible says that she went to where Jesus was, bowed down at the feet of the Master and began to wash His feet with her tears and dry them with her hair. Then she opened up the expensive container of perfume and spilled that fragrant perfume all over the feet of Jesus (Luke 7:38). She worshipped Him because she realized that she had been in the presence of Jesus.

When you know you have been in the presence of the miraculous and the mysterious, you ought to worship Jesus. I remember the 10 lepers who cried out to Jesus for healing. He told them to go and show themselves to the priest. The Bible says that as they were leaving, they were cleansed. Yet, even though all 10 of them were cleansed, only one of them came back and fell at the feet of Jesus and worshiped Him (Luke 17:12-19). Likewise, when you have been in the presence of Jesus and have seen the Lord do some extraordinary things in your life, you've just got to worship Him.

I think of the Gadarene demoniac who had been living in the tombs, cutting himself with sharp stones and crying out in the night. He could not be contained; but when Jesus came by, He exorcised the demon from his life. When the crowd came by, he was sitting down at the feet of Jesus, clothed and in his right mind. When Jesus got back in the boat, he begged to go with Him, but Jesus told him to go home and tell his family about the good things the Lord had done for him (Luke 8:26-39).

You ought to go home today and tell others about the good things the Lord has done for you. If the Lord has been good to you and has blessed your life, if He has brought you back from a long way away, or if you have ever been sick and He healed you, then you ought to tell others about it.

What to Do With Forgiveness
(Matthew 18:21-35)

REV. DR. JEREMIAH TILLMAN

First Baptist Church
Petersburg, Virginia

A South African woman stood in an emotionally charged courtroom listening to white police officers acknowledge the atrocities they had perpetrated in the name of apartheid. Officer Van de Broke acknowledged his responsibility in the death of her son and husband. Along with others, he had shot her 18-year-old son at point-blank range. He and others partied while they burned his body, turning it over on the fire until it was ashes.

Eight years later, Van de Broke and others arrived to seize her husband. Hours later, Van de Broke came back to fetch the woman. He took her to a woodpile where her husband lay bound. She was forced to watch as they poured gasoline over his body and ignited the flames that consumed him. The last words her husband said were, "Forgive them."

Now Van de Broke stood, awaiting judgment. South Africa's Truth and Reconciliation Commission asked the woman what she wanted. "Three things," she said. "I want Mr. Van de Broke to take me to the place where they burned my husband's body. I would like to gather up the dust and give him a decent burial.

"Second, Mr. Van de Broke took all my family away from me, and I still have a lot of love to give. Twice a month, I would like for him to come to the ghetto and spend a day with me so I can be a mother to him.

"Third, I would like Mr. Van de Broke to know that he is forgiven by God and that I forgive him."

In our biblical text, the drama unfolds rapidly, keeping us attentively on the edge of our mental seats. Our feelings are stirred and change rapidly. We feel sympathy for the man who owes such a staggering debt. The king angers us at once because he's going to exact every ounce of life from his debtor. Then abruptly the king is no longer a villain but a hero because of his compassion, and we are flabbergasted at the extent of his mercy. Our anger rises to its highest pitch as the now-forgiven debtor lays hands on a man who owes just pennies and throws him into jail. We breathe a sign of satisfaction, maybe self-righteous satisfaction, when the king brings the unforgiving debtor back to judgment and delivers him to be tormented until his huge, unpayable, mountainous debt is paid.

For Jesus, this drama was one in which we are all participants. He told the story in response to Peter's question, "Lord, how often shall my brother sin against me, and I forgive him? As many as seven times?" Jesus answered him, "I do not say to you seven times, but seventy times seven!" But that wasn't enough for Jesus. He went on to tell the parable of the unforgiving servant to explain what forgiveness is like in the kingdom of heaven.

So Jesus is calling us with this parable to get on the stage ourselves— to recognize that this drama is our life, because nothing is more at the center of life than forgiving and being forgiven.

CHRIST'S RECKONING INCLUDES COMPLETE SETTLING OF ACCOUNTS

In 1992, I returned from Germany as a military chaplain and was assigned to Fort Jackson, South Carolina.

I went to the Department of Motor Vehicles to get a new driver's license. The guy behind the desk said he couldn't help me because my license was suspended.

"There must be some mistake," I said. "I've never done anything to deserve that."

The civil servant was very civil but said I had to clear up the problem with the State of Kentucky before he could help me. I hadn't lived in Kentucky for almost five years, so I couldn't imagine what was wrong. Six long-distance phone calls later, I found out that when I moved from Kentucky, I owed part of an excise tax—two dollars.

That tiny bill began to accrue penalties and interest. I had to pay that bill, plus the cost of a new South Carolina driver's license and registration for a car that had long ago become scrap metal before I could become legal in my new home state. That price tag was nearly $295.

The whole thing was embarrassing. It wasn't so much the money that bothered me; it was knowing that I was on the wrong side of the law for all those years without even being aware of it.

How shocking it will be for those who stand before the God of the universe one day and realize, for the first time, that He holds them accountable for all the wrongs they do.

Note verse 23: "Therefore, the kingdom of heaven is like a king who wanted to settle accounts with his servants." Another translation (RSV) uses the word *reckon*: "Therefore is the kingdom of heaven likened unto a certain king, which would make a *reckoning* with his servants." In this parable, we have a picture of God seeking to reckon with us—each one of us personally, about the matter of our sin and guilt.

There will always be a day of reckoning. Remember the parable of the rich fool (Luke 12:13-21)? The farmer had torn down his barns to build greater barns in order that he might store the bountiful harvest with which he had been blessed. He said to himself, "Soul, take your ease, eat, drink and be merry." But he failed to reckon with the fact that there would be a day of reckoning for him. "Thou fool," God said to him, "this night your soul will be required of you." There will always be a day of reckoning. The inevitable day of reckoning is not just an individual matter; it's a law of life.

One illustration from our national scene will make the point. Washington, D.C. and other cities across the country are facing just such a day of reckoning. Newspapers and television have called our attention to the desperate plight of our economic system: the failing of our financial infrastructure, the meltdown on Wall Street, the failure of our banking systems and the collapse of our housing market. There is and will continue to be a day of reckoning in our community and national life.

The servant in the parable was probably an important official entrusted with considerable financial responsibility, yet he took no initiative in making an accounting to the king. When the time of reckoning came, he was hopelessly in debt.

Likewise, sin poisons our relationship with God. If unattended to, that poison will become so pervasive that our relationship with God will be completely severed. The prophet Isaiah said, "Your iniquities have made a separation between you and your God, and your sins have hid his face from you so that he does not hear" (Isa. 59:2). There will always be a day of reckoning, and every day should be a day of debt-settling.

GOD'S FORGIVENESS IS GREATER THAN OUR SIN

There was a classified ad that read something like this: "LOST— ONE DOG. Brown hair with several mange spots. Right leg broken due to auto accident. Rear left hip hurt. Right eye missing. Left ear bitten off in a dog fight. Answers to name 'Lucky.' Reward to finder."

Lucky? Of course! That was a lucky dog. He was lucky because, even with all those things wrong with him, somebody still wanted him and was willing to pay to get him back. Isn't that the story of the gospel? Despite all of our sin and rebellion, God still loved us enough to pay the ultimate price to win us back to Himself. God's merciful forgiveness is greater than our sin.

Look at the magnitude of the servant's debt in our parable. He owed 10,000 talents. Now that was a large sum of money, more than anybody in ancient Palestine could ever envision. Really, it was sort of like our national debt! The total annual taxes of Judea, Samaria, Galilee and Berea, according to George Buttrick, amounted to only 800 talents.

So when we read of a 10,000-talent debt, we're not talking about something that could be paid off with a home-improvement loan. We're talking about megabucks!

It was part of Jesus' style of teaching to exaggerate to make a point. We call it hyperbole. Ten thousand was the highest number used in reckoning and the talent was the largest currency unit of the time. Therefore, 10,000 talents represented a debt that humanly speaking was impossible ever to repay. In a dramatic way, Jesus is telling us that we owe God a debt that we can never repay. But God's love is like the mercy of a king who would forgive a debt of 10,000 talents.

This was the first biblical bail-out in biblical history. This man was more than likely a big-time CEO working on Wall Street in downtown Jerusalem, when he was bailed out by the government (the king). Whether it was 10,000 talents or 700 billion dollars, this man did not have the capacity to pay either amount!

You know what that means? It means that God's love is abundant enough to cover every moral debt that any mortal owes. You need never worry about your shortcomings or your sins in terms of the adequacy of God's grace to forgive them. God's forgiveness is greater than your sin.

How much of the heartache and devastating guilt that cripples and debilitates people would be done away with if people would believe that God's love is deep enough and wide enough to forgive—and to forgive to the utmost? Don't forget it! God's merciful forgiveness is greater than our sin.

FORGIVENESS MUST BE PART OF TRUE CHRISTIANITY

There is a story that is told about the great artist, Leonardo da Vinci. While da Vinci labored on his masterpiece, "The Last Supper," he became angry with another man. They quarreled, with da Vinci hurling bitter accusations and threats at the other fellow. Returning to his canvas, the artist attempted to paint the face of Jesus but found that he was unable to do so. He was so upset that he could not compose himself for the painstaking work. Finally, he set down his brushes, sealed his paint pots and went to search for the man with whom he had argued. He apologized and asked for forgiveness, which his antagonist graciously gave. Only then was da Vinci able to return to his workshop and complete the face of the Savior. Forgiveness must be a part of what it means to be a Christian.

The servant who owed 10,000 talents had fallen on his knees before the king and begged, "Lord, have patience with me, and I will pay you everything." Of course, there was no possible way he could repay such a debt, but the king took pity on him and forgave his debt. But no sooner had this man been forgiven his debt than he went out and found a fellow servant who was indebted to him. However, instead of owing 10,000 talents, this man owed only 100 denarii, about 20 cents. Once again, Jesus exaggerated to make a point. This was a debt that could have been repaid easily to a patient creditor.

Now, get the picture! The man who had just gotten a reprieve from absolute poverty and life imprisonment seized his fellow servant by the throat and said, "Give me the 20 cents you owe me." And his fellow servant begged, "Have patience with me, and I will pay you." Surely those words had a familiar ring! But when the money was not repaid immediately, the man had his fellow servant thrown in prison. No wonder the other servants were greatly distressed and reported what had happened to their lord! We have here a picture of a man without gratitude for his lord's forgiveness and without compassion for his fellow human beings—one suffering from what the Bible describes as hardness of heart.

When the king learned that the very one who had been forgiven a debt of 10,000 talents refused to forgive a debt of 100 denarii, the king had the servant thrown into prison. Jesus concludes, "So, also, my Heavenly Father will do to everyone of you if you do not forgive your brother from your heart" (v. 35).

Don't forget it! Forgiveness must be a part of what it means to be a Christian. ❧

The Paradox of Our Predicament
(2 Corinthians 4:7-15)

REV. DR. MAURICE WATSON

Beulahland Bible Church
Macon, Georgia

Hanns Sachs, in his book, *Masks of Love and Life,* tells the story of two brothers. The younger brother had a fear of open doors. The older brother became impatient and wanted to break him of his habit, so he threatened him by saying, "One day I will lock you up in a room with all the doors opened."

Those of us who have answered the call of gospel ministry and Christian service for any length of time have perhaps discovered that we often feel like we are "locked in a room with open doors." The truth of the matter is that we can choose to leave the ministry at any time. No one holds a gun to our heads, daring us not to quit! But most of us feel compelled and obligated to tread on in Christian ministry despite the pain, problems and pressures that inherently come with it. Yes, it seems that we are locked in a room with open doors.

We are trapped and incarcerated by a calling that, on one hand, we cannot escape; but, on the other hand, we can walk away from it. It appears that we are residents in what Pete Rose appropriately called his autobiography, *My Prison Without Bars.* We are "locked in a room with open doors," "residents in a 'prison without bars,' " and "captured by a calling that we are free to leave." These are such paradoxical notions, aren't they? They seem to be so contradictory, so absurd and so nonsensical. But if we are honest with ourselves, they get at the very essence of our predicament.

Why do we put up with the headaches and heartaches that Christian ministry sometimes causes us to experience? Is it the money? Perhaps it is for some, but most ministers are underpaid; and many others have the skills to enjoy a more lucrative lifestyle doing something else. Is it a desire to have prestige and power? Perhaps for some, but many of us have long since gotten beyond that ego-need. Is it because we are masochists who enjoy pain? No, I would give even the few among us who have the greatest need to be a victim more credit than that. So why do we continue to put up with tests, trials and troubles of a ministry that we could walk away from? Does it not have to do with the paradoxical nature of our predicament?

I am reminded of a book I read several years ago that described a personality disorder with which some people suffer. The title of the book is *I Hate You, Don't Leave Me*. It describes a person who is a "walking contradiction" and a "living paradox." When one tries to make sense of our rationale for remaining in the ministry despite its difficulties, we must look like "walking contradictions" and "living paradoxes."

No person was ever more aware of the paradoxical nature of Christianity than the apostle Paul. Listen to Paul as, over and over again, he employs this rhetorical tool of language in which he juxtaposes two seemingly contrasting notions in order to highlight an eternal truth. He told the Galatians that they had been called to freedom, but they were to "serve" (word used for slavery) one another (Gal. 5:13)—that's a paradox! He told the Christians in Rome that they were to be "living sacrifices" (Rom. 12:1)—that's a paradox! He told the Corinthians, "When I am weak, then I am strong" (2 Cor. 12:10)—that's a paradox! He told the Ephesians to "walk in wisdom," (Eph. 5:15) but he told the Corinthians, "I'm a fool for Christ" (2 Cor. 11:23)—that's a paradox!

Here in our text, Paul once again uses this tool of language as he defends his apostolic authority. He was the founding pastor of a difficult church in Corinth, which had been infiltrated by people who were challenging his authority as an apostle. If you think you have a difficult pastoral assignment, imagine yourself trying to pastor a church in which rumors were circulating suggesting that you only preach for your aggrandizement. Imagine how hurt you would be if you wrote a letter to that church indicating your intention to pay them a visit, but they sent word back to you saying that they would rather you not come. Imagine how you would feel if you heard the members saying, "He writes well, but he can't preach!" Imagine how insulted you would be if you knew that many of the members did not want you to be their pastor because you didn't have an impressive physical appearance.

Why did Paul not walk away from a church like this? Rather than retreating, he defended his honor and authority as an apostle by writing this second letter to the Corinthians. Even the way Paul responded to his critics in this letter was paradoxical. He did not defend himself by extolling his credentials. He did not build a case for his apostleship by highlighting his educational background, his extensive travels and his theological prowess. If I were the pastor of a church like this and they challenged my authority, I would be tempted to maximize myself in their sight by reminding them of my pastoral experience and educational qualifications! Paul built his case, rather, by "minimizing" himself. He defended himself not by *extolling* his strengths, but by exposing his weaknesses!

Are you secure enough in your walk with God to minimize your sense of greatness because you understand that it's really not about you? That's what Paul does in this letter. He has a healthy self-understanding of who he is in the scheme of God's redemptive plan.

In paradoxical form, he maximizes the greatness of the glorious gospel that he preaches, but he also minimizes himself. He challenges us to have a healthy self-understanding of the paradoxical nature of our predicament.

WE ARE POWERFUL WEAKLINGS

After highlighting the fact that the glorious gospel that we preach is greater than even the glory of Moses' revelation on Mt. Sinai, Paul underscores who we are in the total scheme of things. He says, "We preach a glorious gospel (which he describes as the 'light of the knowledge of the glory of God in the face of Jesus Christ'—v. 6), but we have this treasure in earthen vessels" (v. 7).

Earthen vessels were common clay pots or jars that were found all over Jerusalem in the first century. Paul does not refer to exquisite, expensive fine china, but to clay pots that perhaps had cracks, chips and holes in them. The contrast (paradox) that he highlights is between the great expense of the treasure (the gospel) and the cheapness of the container (clay pots). The contrast is between the indispensable treasure and the dispensable container—the power of the treasure and the fragility of the container.

The paradox is that God would entrust something so powerful, something so precious and valuable in something so fragile and easy to break. We talk a lot about our trust in God, but does not this text seem to imply that God trusts us? Think about it. That which we value the most, we try to keep safe. We value our families, so we provide them a home in a safe neighborhood. We value our money; therefore, we deposit it in a bank in order to keep it safe. We put important papers in a fireproof safe. Nuclear weapons are kept in hardened containers in order to keep them safe.

But look at the apparent absurdity of God! He places his most valued possession (the light of His glory in the face of Jesus Christ) in clay jars—cracked pots! In a sense, that's all we are as preachers of the gospel—cracked pots!

I was drinking some water recently, when I noticed that the glass was cracked and chipped. Without thinking twice, I threw the glass away. You see, we throw away things that are cracked and broken, but God is looking for people who are cracked, broken and weak! The amazing thing is that God would entrust something so powerful in something so fragile and weak. Cracked pots, that's all we are—fragile and weak!

Paul explains why God places His precious gospel in weak vessels— "that the excellence of the power may be of God and not of us" (v. 7b). Let's be clear about it; we are not the source of the power we possess. Whatever power we have is not derived from us; instead, we have received it from God. Paul is telling us that while the gospel we preach is powerful, we who preach it are weak. We are powerful weaklings!

WE ARE WOUNDED SURVIVORS

In a telling series of antitheses, Paul offers insights of his self-evaluation. He gives some illustrations that indicate just how weak we are, but he also shows us how powerful the gospel is by reminding us that although we are *wounded*, we are still *survivors*!

Keep in mind that Paul's apostolic authority was being questioned and challenged, and he defended himself as an apostle. However, he didn't defend himself by highlighting his *accomplishments*. Rather, he defended himself by highlighting his *afflictions*. Paul suggested that part of the proof of the authenticity of his apostleship had to do with the fact that he had not quit the ministry, despite the struggles that he faced. In the text, Paul essentially says, "The reason you can know that my apostleship is real is because I didn't give up! I didn't quit in spite of the afflictions that I faced!"

Paul encourages us not to be in denial concerning the trouble that we face as ministers of the gospel. He admits the fact that there are many struggles we have to deal with on a daily basis. In an antiphonal fashion, he shouts out what happens to us; but he shouts back what didn't happen to us, and the inference is that what didn't happen, should have happened! He draws a contrast between our pain and our perseverance—between our suffering and our survival. In each case, he uses the conjunction "yet" or "but" to connect what happened to us with what didn't happen to us. On the left side of the conjunction he says, "We are *wounded*," but on the right side of the conjunction he says, "We are *survivors*!"

Listen to Paul as he gives another antiphonal report of our predicament. In verse 8, he shouts out, "We are hard pressed on every side," but he shouts back, "yet not crushed!" He shouts out, "We are perplexed," but he shouts back, "but not in despair!" He shouts out, "We are persecuted," but he shouts back, "but not forsaken!" He shouts out, "We are struck down," but he shouts back, "but we are not destroyed!"

Paul is saying that the side of the conjunction on which we choose to live determines the proof of our calling. If we reside only on the left side of the conjunction, we would become narcissistic, fatalistic and hopeless. We would be driven to doubt and despair our calling, and we would walk away from the ministry forever! This happens when our focus is one-sided—when we focus only on the left side of the conjunction where our wounds are exposed. My prayer is that this sermon will help to push our faith to the right side of "but" and remind us that while we are *wounded*, we are *survivors*!

WE ARE DYING LIFE-GIVERS

In a strange paradox, Paul portrays the union between the suffering that we go through for the sake of the gospel and the suffering that Jesus endured on the cross. He juxtaposes two diametrically opposite terms—"death" and "life" in order to highlight the fact that we are *dying life-givers.*

In verses 10-12, the repetitive use of these two opposite terms, "death" and "life," suggests that they serve as bookends of the life of a gospel preacher. Paul says we are "always carrying about in the body the *dying* of the Lord Jesus, that the *life* of Jesus also may be manifested in our mortal flesh" (emphasis mine). He is saying, "Every day that I wake up to minister, I start the new day facing the possibility that I may die for Christ! Every day I face danger, cruelties, insults and enemies who want me dead!" And we go through all of this so that "the life of Jesus may be manifested in our body."

The paradox is that we are ministers of *life*, but we carry *death* in our bodies. Paul is telling us that we are dying life-givers. He explicitly states it in verse 12: "So then death is working in us, but life in you." *The Message Bible* says, "While we're going through the worst, you're getting in on the best!" In other words, what's killing us is giving life to others! We are dying life-givers. That's the paradox of our predicament.

May we take heart in knowing that we share the same predicament that Jesus faced in His ministry. He also was a *powerful weakling*. He was powerful enough to be God, but He was also weak enough to become a man. He was powerful enough to give the woman at the well eternal water, but He was also weak enough to declare on the cross, "I thirst."

Like each of us, Jesus was a *wounded survivor*. He was wounded for our transgressions and bruised for our iniquities. On Friday, He was wounded on the cross, but on Sunday a resurrected Lord could declare, "I survived!"

Finally, He was a *dying life-giver*. He died in order to give life to those who were dead in trespasses and sins! His predicament was the same as ours—a paradox!

Hanns Sachs, *Masks of Love and Life* (Cambridge, Mass.: Science-Art Publishers, 1948), 54.

No Longer Left Alone:
A Sermon Excerpt from *Left Alone*
(John 14:15-18)

‿◦⊱✿⊰◦‿

PASTOR RALPH DOUGLAS WEST SR.

The Church Without Walls
Houston, Texas

General Douglas MacArthur forged a bond with the people of the Philippine Islands during the Second World War. Throughout the conflict, he promised them his loyalty. The general kept his word, remaining with them at the risk of his life, staying on even when Japanese forces attacked the islands heavily.

President Franklin Roosevelt eventually ordered MacArthur to leave the Philippines in 1942. Against his wishes, the general packed, gathered his family and got into a boat to make his way to Australia. Before he departed, he made the famous statement, "I shall return." MacArthur also kept that promise.

Jesus also spoke of His return. In John 14:18, He tells His disciples that He will not leave them alone. He says that His followers won't be treated like orphans. Those words are just as comforting and inspiring for us today as they were for the disciples who walked with our Lord. Jesus keeps His promises.

When our hearts are troubled, when we're weighed down by life, when we're struggling with anxiety, having Jesus near is a soothing balm. The verses that we'll examine in John 14 have been encouraging to me. When I feel like I've been left alone, when I feel like no one understands my troubles and my circumstances, they remind me that I'm still in God's presence. That's reassuring.

Look at these promises from Jesus. Hear anew how our Lord comes to the weak. Hear again about the promised Holy Spirit. Hear how His strength and power can give the energy that we so desperately need to face the difficulties of this life.

Let's look at John 14:15-18: "If you love me, keep my commandments. And I will pray the Father, and he shall give you another helper that he may abide with you forever. The Spirit of truth, whom the world cannot receive, because it neither sees him nor knows him, but you know him for he dwells with you and will be in you. I will not leave you orphans. I will come to you."

These words are the farewell discourse of Jesus to His disciples. The disciples had grown accustomed to Jesus being with them. As He began speaking to them as described in John 14, their hearts were breaking because they now understood that He was leaving. When they heard these words, the contours of their faces shifted, their expressions changed and their hearts were saddened by the possibility of His absence. Jesus takes this opportunity to remind them that He cannot be everywhere and with everyone. He explains that it's expedient for Him to leave so that He can expand His presence and be with everyone, everywhere, at the same time.

Imagine if Jesus had said, "I'm going to Jerusalem." Every time we wanted to communicate with Him, we'd have to take a trans-Atlantic flight. We'd have to travel to Tel Aviv, go to the Holy Land, find Jesus and get an appointment. Thankfully, Jesus didn't go to Jerusalem. He returned to the Father so that He's available in a manner that enables him to be everywhere at the same time. It means that He can be with me in Houston, with brothers in New York, sisters in California, churches in South America, in Europe and in Africa at the same time. There's no loss of His presence; it's not like spotty cell phone coverage. Jesus is available everywhere with the same dynamic presence.

People who want to pay homage to the memory of Napoleon can go to Paris and visit the cathedral that has his wonderful casket. People who want to see the sarcophagus of the Duke of Wellington will go to St. Paul's Church in England. Patriots interested in the lives of past presidents might travel to Springfield, Illinois, and visit the tomb of Abraham Lincoln. Those who want to remember civil rights leaders go to Atlanta to the tomb of Martin Luther King Jr. But when we want to worship Jesus, we don't need to travel long distances. Because of the Holy Spirit, Jesus is with us right now.

I've been amazed at the number of Christians who are not informed about these basics of the Holy Spirit, who seemed to have skipped this portion of Christianity 101. Too many have only heard about the Holy Spirit; they've never taken the time to examine what the Scriptures actually say. When they hear about the Holy Spirit, it's from someone who gave too much inaccurate information. They hear people saying that the Holy Ghost got them clapping, running and shouting. There are plenty of other things that can make you behave that way.

When Jesus says the Father will send "another helper," the words that He uses tell us how this helper comes and what He does. Let's look more closely at some of the words that the Scriptures use to describe the Holy Spirit.

In John 14, Jesus says that He will ask the Father to give *another helper*. In the original language, those words—*Allas Proroleton*—mean "one of the same kind." Jesus doesn't use the words *Heteross Proroleton*, which would mean "of another kind." He specifically chooses words to communicate that the helper that He sends will be just like Him.

Here's what Jesus was saying: "I will ask the Father to give you another, someone who is exactly the same as I am. In My absence, this helper will be for you what I've been when I was present. The Holy Spirit will be what I was when we were together at the Sea of Galilee, in the city of Capernaum, and in Jerusalem. Whatever I did, the Holy Spirit will do. Even though I'm going away, you won't lose anything that you experienced when I was present."

In some translations, the verses in John 14 refer to the Holy Spirit as *another comforter*. Don't mistake the word "comforter" to be something passive. In our English nomenclature, *comfort* suggests something that's weak, romantic, fuzzy and soft. But the original language uses a military term that carries the notion of support and strength. In that context, "comfort" means that when our hearts are troubled, when we are weak and beside ourselves, He will come alongside to provide support. He will lay His hands on our shoulders, providing us with strength and power. He's going to tell us that He's walking with us through the valley, through the shadow of death and disappointment.

Sometimes, the Holy Spirit is described as *another advocate*. John also writes that "We have a mediator between God and man, an advocate that makes intercession for us" (1 John 2:1). He also implies that this one who is to come, the Holy Spirit, will plead on our behalf. He will be one who will plead our case before the cosmic courts. We have somebody who will represent us; our advocate will plead our case.

In some places, the Holy Spirit is *another counselor*. John 14:26 tells us that as a counselor, the Holy Spirit will teach us all things and remind us of everything that Jesus said. When we're confused, He'll straighten us out; He'll be our counselor.

The Father provided another. We have another who is just like Jesus. After their biological mother put them up for adoption, two identical twin boys were put in different homes and separated for 39 years. After years of searching, the brothers found each other. They became known as the "Jim twins."

Jim Lewis said that meeting his identical twin brother, Jim Springer, was like looking in a mirror. Although they'd been apart for nearly four decades, they discovered an enormous number of similarities. Both Jims:

- Had been adopted by families from Ohio
- Were named "Jim" by their adoptive parents
- As boys, had a dog named "Toy," were nail-biters, fretful sleepers and suffered from migraine headaches
- Married twice. Their first wives were both named Linda; their second wives were both named Betty.
- Had sons. One was named "Jim Allen;" the other was Jim Alan.
- Smoked Salem cigarettes, drank Miller Lite beer, loved stock-car racing and hated baseball
- Built children's furniture in the basement and constructed circular white benches around the trees in their backyards
- Had the same IQ, nearly the same heartbeat pattern, brain waves, and nearly identical handwriting
- Died on the same day

When Jesus said, "one of the same kind," He meant that He and the Holy Spirit were even more identical than Jim and Jim. There's absolutely no difference between them. Everything that Jesus did, the Holy Spirit is doing.

I wish more of us could appreciate the person and the presence of the Holy Spirit. Without the Holy Spirit, we cannot witness, and we cannot know the truth. He's the one who guides us. He's our counselor, our teacher and the one who instructs us. We need the power of the Holy Spirit to be functional believers.

In a very real sense, Jesus now comes to us in a more powerful and dynamic way than He ever did in the past. Verse 17 tells us, "The Spirit of truth, whom the world cannot receive, because it neither sees Him nor knows Him, but you know Him for He dwells with you and will be in you."

Up until this moment, the God of the Old Testament had been with Israel, dwelling in clouds, in tabernacles and temples and in the Ark of the Covenant. He had been with them in budded rods, He had been with them in stone tablets and He had come to them through sacrificial offerings and covenant regulations. When Jesus Christ came, the God who was far off had come near. The word became flesh and dwelt among us.

When Jesus was about to leave, He explained how much closer He would dwell. He said, "I will not leave you alone. I will give you another just like me—the spirit of truth. You will know him because you have known me. He will be **with** you—but also *in* you."

Jesus had been with His disciples on multiple occasions, and they had seen Him demonstrate His power. He wants the church to know that because the Holy Spirit came, Jesus has established residence inside of us. Jesus is with us now in the same way that He had been with His disciples in the past.

We shouldn't be astonished when we hear of God working miracles today. It shouldn't baffle our minds. The same Jesus who worked miracles then is working them today. In fact, the Scriptures say that we will do greater works than those that were done in the past. We ought to be witnessing something more dynamic and different because the Holy Spirit lives within us. If the church really believed that, we couldn't build buildings large enough for the multitudes that would come.

In addition to being **with** us, Jesus says that He's also *in* us. He dwells within, He's become part of our very essence, and He uses our hands and our feet. That's what Paul spoke about in Galatians. He said, "I'm a new man in Christ—Christ is in me. And now the life that I live is no longer mine. It's the life of Christ, who's in me" (Gal. 2:20).

Albert Einstein was on the cover of *Time* magazine recently, when he was posthumously named the Person of the Century. Einstein grew up in a nominally Jewish home and was later exposed to religion through the Catholic church. He later abandoned his faith, thinking that it interfered with science and reason. In his fifties, he returned to his Jewish roots. An interviewer asked him his thoughts on Jesus, wondering what Albert Einstein thought about people who claim this Jesus was the Christ. Standing in his laboratory, Einstein said, "Anyone who reads the New Testament and meets Jesus on its pages leaves understanding he's more real in this laboratory than he was 2,000 years ago."

In verse 18, Jesus says, "I will not leave you orphans. I will come to you." That word "orphans" is only used in one other place, which is James 1:27. Scholars have not given a strict definition of what that word means, but it's safe to assume that it's saying that we won't be left fatherless.

Since fathers provide resources, this verse communicates that God will provide whatever we need when the Holy Spirit comes to us. As you're reading this, pause and ask yourself what you need from God. I'm not talking about some "cheap-trinket Christianity." I'm not talking about cars, adding more square footage to your house, or some new clothes. The things that we need from God are those things that money cannot buy.

What we need is peace. The peace that the Holy Spirit brings—the "shalom" of God—is what miraculously puts us back together when we're falling apart. We also need joy, which many people confuse with happiness. Happiness is situational: we're happy that we have a job, a boyfriend or a girlfriend. If you need someone or something to make you happy, that's not joy. Joy comes from abiding with God; it's in His presence that we find fullness of joy.

Sometimes, it is good to be left alone. It might not appear that way initially, but in hindsight, we can see how it's benefited us. In John 16:7-8, Jesus explained to His disciples how His leaving would help them: "But I tell you the truth: It is for your good that I am going away. Unless I go away, the Counselor will not come to you; but if I go, I will send Him to you."

Jesus wasn't going away to bring sadness upon His followers; He was leaving so that they would never be alone again. He would dwell within them, walking even closer and in a much more dynamic manner.

Our Lord tried to tell them about the Holy Spirit, but they didn't quite get it. They scratched their heads when Jesus said, "In a little while you will see Me no more, and then after a little while you will see Me." The disciples wouldn't understand what Jesus was talking about until Pentecost.

The very essence of the Christian experience shouts that Jesus hasn't left us alone. "Christ in you," writes Paul, "the hope of glory." Because God dwells closer to us than ever before, we are no longer alone.

I Want to Be a Representative
(Ezekiel 2:1-10)

❧

REV. RALPH D. WEST II

The Church Without Walls
Houston, Texas

Fifty stars, 13 stripes and three colors assembled together represent the motif of the American flag. The stars symbolize the 50 states, and the 13 stripes signify the first 13 colonies that revolted against the British Crown. Red is for valor, white is for purity and blue points to the heavenly sky as the destination that all of us aspire to rest.

Throughout the world, the flag is used in public discourse to refer to the United States—not only as a nation, government and set of policies—but also as an ideology or set of ideas. Many understand the flag to represent the freedoms and rights guaranteed in the U.S. Constitution and its Bill of Rights and, perhaps most of all, to symbolize individual and personal liberty as set forth in the Declaration of Independence.

When non-believers and believers alike see and hear you, do they witness a representative of Christ—or His opposition? How can we represent the faith and the God we proclaim to believe in? This text is tailored to teach us that *we can be representatives of the Lord when our life is a sign pointing to the Savior.*

THE RIGHT POSITION FOR HEARING GOD'S VOICE

Ezekiel has just witnessed the glory of the Lord: the four creatures, the four wheels and the Lord seated on His throne. In this strange land of Babylon, His glory is testifying that His present, active power is not determined by circumstances.

At the age of 30, this is the year when he would be ordained to become a priest. God tells him, "Son of man, stand on your feet, and I will speak to you." He falls to his face in the first chapter as a priest but then stands on his feet in the second chapter as a prophet. When the Lord speaks, His word transforms. "Stand on your feet" is a command for him to be prepared for his future challenges. The direction of his life has been completely transformed for an assignment designed for a prophet. His foundation has been strengthened to withstand the tests that he would face in his ministry. Likewise, you too can have this strength and experience His transformation when you *put yourself in a position to hear His voice.*

The River Chebar was the place where the faithful Israelites would go to pray and worship. In the same way, you give God the opportunity to break in on you and reveal His presence when you put yourself in the position of prayer and devotion.

His firm foundation has prepared him for the direction that the Lord is sending him: "Son of man, I am sending you to the children of Israel, to a rebellious nation that has rebelled against Me; they and their fathers have transgressed against Me to this very day."

DON'T GET LOST!

The history of the Israelites was that of a people who were consistently sinful. In the account recorded in Exodus 32, the Israelites built a golden calf soon after their deliverance from the clutches of the Egyptians. Numbers 25 says they were whoring with other gods, turning from the Lord. The Lord then referred to the Israelites as "the nation," a description normally ascribed to the Gentiles. Their sinful nature and weak foundation caused the separation. **When you don't follow God's directions, you are bound to get lost.**

During my senior year in high school, my friend Kalani Wear and I took our lady friends on a double date to the homecoming dance. Afterward, we had to take them home, and they both lived on opposite sides of Houston. We drove all over the city trying to find our way back home, even though the whole time we had a cell phone. We just would not call my father and ask him for directions.

In the same way, the Israelites would not ask the Lord for His direction but decided instead to depend on their own knowledge, beliefs and way. *When you don't follow God's directions, you are bound to get lost.*

As a senior at Westfield High School, I was so excited about Homecoming that I disregarded my father's specific instructions to call him after the event and ask for directions home. Even though I was a Houston resident, I was unfamiliar with the city. I took my date home after the dance but still worried about how I would get home. I was determined to get home without any help, but I failed miserably. I drove around the city for three hours and was on a fourth of a tank of gas before I got home. The entire time I had the cellular phone in my cup holder, but I wanted to do things my own way.

The children of Israel had access to the Lord whenever they needed His help. They were a strong-willed people who decided to live their lives independent of God. The Lord referred to the children of Israel not as "my children" but as "them, they and those." They are identified no longer as personal possessions but as individuals divided and apart from Him. Likewise, our sinful decision to live by our own human will causes definite separation from God.

The Lord gives us a spiritual cardiac diagnosis of their condition: "They are impudent and stubborn children." The Old Testament defines their heart or will to be the central part of their violation. They were motivated by a fixed, stubborn self-will that dismissed the will and Word of God. Their hearts were unyielding. They were like a man found guilty in a court of law who completely disregards the verdict. Their impudent boldness caused them to act out the desires of their hearts, expressed through their actions and words.

IS YOUR LIFE A SIGNPOST FOR GOD?

Ezekiel was sent to Israel to tell them, "Thus says the Lord God." He would be identified as a prophet by what he said. The mission of the prophet was to speak to the will of man on behalf of God. If Ezekiel was identified by what he said, then what should be the content of our conversation?

Charles H. Spurgeon wrote a sermon on "Revival" and challenged his congregation to engage in Christian conversation: "Pay attention to the conversation of the average professing Christian. You might spend from the beginning of January to the end of December and never hear them speak about their faith. They will scarcely even mention the name of Jesus Christ at all. On Sunday afternoon, what will they talk about at the dinner table? It will not be about the minister's sermon, unless they want to point out some faults. We talk too little about the Lord. Many of us need to pray, 'O Lord, revive Your work in my soul, that my conversation may be more about Christ, seasoned with salt, and kept by the Holy Spirit.'"

The Lord tells Ezekiel to speak—even if they did not listen or ignored what he said. At first, it seems like there is hope in God's message to Israel, but the seventh verse of the third chapter says that the people would not listen at all. If his message identified him as a prophet and they still wouldn't listen, then how would they know for sure he was a prophet?

A recent article in *Reader's Digest* featured church signs across America, such as "Keep using My name in vain and I'll make rush hour long," "Don't give up! Moses was once a basket case!" and "Let's meet at my house Sunday before the game, signed God." Each sign arrested my attention: I could understand its message even though there was no voice to go with it! The indication is clear that signs speak for themselves. The Lord wanted Ezekiel's life to be a sign. *As a sign, his life was to speak louder than what he had to say.*

Ezekiel needed to be alerted of some struggles that were awaiting him in the future. The people would not listen. They would be rebellious and bring much pain to his ministry. His ministry would be filled with pain and scar him deeply. He would have to live among people who were compared to thorns and scorpions. Why would the Lord put His prophet among thorns and scorpions?

When I lived in Birmingham, Alabama, I noticed several hills and unlit, sharp corners marked by signs that said, "Beware of the curves." The Woodlands, Texas, my current residence, has a plentiful variety of wildlife, so there are signs that say, "Watch for deer." In high-traffic areas, four-way stop signs and lights are always present. Every sign has been placed in a location where there is potential danger. *God wanted Ezekiel to be a sign warning the people of the dangerous outcome of their sinful actions if they didn't repent.*

LIVING WITH SCORPIONS AND THORNS

Why then did the prophet have to live in the midst of scorpions and thorns? It evokes the picture of a man waking up early in the morning and running barefoot through a field of thorns cutting his legs and feet. When he reaches the end of the field, everywhere that he is walking are scorpions in attack position anticipating his every move. (Thorns pierce, cut and damage the flesh. Scorpions, by nature, pierce their prey with the intention of crippling, paralyzing or killing so they can consume it.) This hostile climate was where he was to live and preach.

When my brother Ralpheal and I were wrestling in the house two years ago, he scratched my arm. Ralpheal still has a scar on his hand from the time I increased the speed on the treadmill when we were kids in St. Louis. I have noticed that every scratch and scar points to the time and place of its origin. It may be possible that one of the signs that would be used as a symbol for the people would be Ezekiel's scars and pain while he obeyed the Lord. John 16:33 says, "In Me you will have peace, in the world you will have tribulations; but be of good cheer, I have overcome the world."

Why would the Lord put His prophet among thorns and scorpions? *It's possible that God wanted Ezekiel to focus on the assignment and not the outcome.* If you focus on the outcome and not the task, you begin to worry, so you are led into sin. In Matthew 6:25, Jesus says, "Therefore don't worry about your life." If you focus on the task, however, it will keep you in God's will. The faithful witness of His message was more important than a successful response.

YOU ARE WHAT YOU EAT

Ezekiel was told where he would go, what to say, how to live and what to expect. God was telling him what he would be able to do in the future, but he required a final ingredient for the present. Everything that the Lord had given to the prophet was exactly what the people of Israel had rejected. They no longer had the strength of His Spirit. This was why their foundation was weak and they had fallen into temptation. Israel had not followed God's directions, so they had been lost in sin. Their hearts were corrupt, and their actions identified them as rebels and not His children.

In the ninth verse, Ezekiel said, "Now when I looked, there was a hand stretched out to me; and behold, a scroll of a book was on it." God told him four times to eat the scroll: "Open your mouth and eat." He wanted the prophet to accept the word: "Eat what you find." The prophet had to read the word: "Eat the word and speak it." He had to recite the word and make it a part of his daily conversation: "Eat this scroll and fill your stomach with it." He wanted the prophet to live on the word.

At Gold's Gym, the nutritionist has a booth set up specifically for dietary counsel. I asked him why it is so important that we maintain such a strict diet. The nutritionist told the class that you are what you eat.

If God's word is in you, then it will come out of you. If His word is in your heart, it will show in your actions even when you don't speak.

The content of Ezekiel's message was lamentation, mourning and woe. Laments were normally funeral songs written in Hebrew poetic form that were sung in times of bereavement. Mournings were words uttered by a bereaved family member mourning the death of a loved one. Woe was an exclamation of distress about a great loss of any kind. But when the prophet tasted the scroll, it was like sweetness in his mouth. The content was bad, but the taste was so good. The bad news was only bad because the good news was so good. What was the good news about the content that was given by the hand of God?

GOD ALWAYS EXTENDS HIS HAND

My family spent three weeks in Europe during the summer of 2008. We visited Oxford, London, Paris and Dublin. Exiting the plane in Ireland, there was a bus awaiting us to transport the passengers to the baggage claim area. While riding on the bus, I noticed a father who was having some difficulties with his son receiving his instructions. He persistently told his son to hold on to him so that he would not lose his balance on the ride, but he refused to do so. When the bus began moving toward its destination, the child lost his footing and was falling to the floor, but before he hit the ground his father caught him by the wrist. He pulled his son back onto his feet and told him, "I told you to hold on to me."

The good news is that even though the children of Israel were rebelling against the Lord, He never stopped extending His hand. This was a love letter to His children warning them that if they did not obey Him, they would experience destruction.

The good news is that the Lord has given us a warning in His Son Jesus Christ. Ezekiel was a sign, but the "Way" has now come. Even though God put his word into flesh with Ezekiel, John 1:14 says, "His word became flesh and dwelled among us." God also gave us His loving warning in John 3:16: "God so loved the world that He gave His only Son, that whoever believes in Him would not perish but have everlasting life." In John 14:6, God warned His people again through Jesus: "I am the way, the truth and the life. No one comes to the Father but through Me." God's warning also came through the apostle Paul in Romans 10:9: "If you confess with your mouth that Jesus is Lord and believe in your heart that God raised Him from the dead, you will be saved."

The good news is that if you accept the warning, you can say with the Psalmist, "Oh, taste and see that the Lord is good" (Ps. 34:8). If you accept the warning, you can sing with every believer, "Amazing grace, how sweet the sound/That saved a wretch like me/ I once was lost/ But now am found."

What Lies Beneath
(Psalm 51:6)

BISHOP KENNETH WHITE

Linconia Tabernacle Christian Center
Trevose, Pennsylvania

God is not interested in what you are on the surface. You may be baptized but still be nothing more than a baptized, unsaved sinner. You may be a member of a church; but, my friend, that is all exterior. You may still be lost! God says that He desires truth in the inside.

Psalm 51 is associated with one of the hardest experiences of David's life, the aftermath of his affair with Bathsheba. This is one of several psalms of David in which the title specifies the incident that inspired the poem. The following thoughts describe David's life journey as God uncovers the unfavorable intent of his heart and gently allows grace and mercy to lead him along the pathway to repentance. As you read, keep in mind that sin was found in David from the beginning. From birth he was inclined toward sin (Rom. 5:12); but where sin abounded, grace abounded much more (Rom. 5:20).

That same grace is available to you today. This Bible story is a caricature of many people whom we know and love or maybe even an example of where you are today. Prayerfully, you can take in the information herewith and allow the grace and mercy of God to uncover "the real you" and change your life from the inside out. *Inward parts* is a rare term in the Hebrew Bible, indicating that something is clouded over or difficult for anyone to see, except God. The Lord's penetrating gaze searches the innermost recesses of a person's mind and heart.

THE REAL PERSON

Approximately a year ago, I spoke to the congregation at Linconia Tabernacle Christian Center in Trevose, Pennsylvania, concerning "Extreme Makeovers." Stemming from a popular television program that features radical alterations in the outward appearances of its guests, this theme forced me to see how much time and effort is put into changing the outward appearance while nothing is being done internally.

In 2 Timothy 3:5, the apostle Paul speaks of "…having a form of godliness, but denying the power thereof." Another translation of this verse reads, "They'll make a show of religion, but behind the scenes they are like animals" (MSG). God used that particular version to gain my attention and steer my focus toward the internal things. I soon began to ask myself the question, *"What lies beneath?"*

One of the first things that came to mind involved the years that I spent as a juvenile probation officer. Many times, the young men and women to whom I was assigned would appear to be sorrowful and remorseful because of their decision to commit crime; but in reality, they were just sorry they got caught. Sadly, even after much counsel, a large percentage would become repeat offenders, involving themselves in the same criminal behavior or perhaps something even worse. There was the pretense of change, but no evidence of any long-term psychological adjustment. The change was only an outward façade that was carefully positioned to disguise what really lay beneath. The *real person*, the one underneath all of the polite greetings and well-placed mannerisms, is always the one who shows up in a pinch. It is all too easy for people to be fooled; but it has been my experience that if you just wait, the *real person* will surface. No matter how harmless the person may appear, the evil nature that has been concealed will always be uncovered.

THE CAMOUFLAGE

Many people have become good at hiding the real person. As a matter of fact, you can find almost anything to help camouflage the real you. Hair weaves and wigs, inflated and enhanced body parts (not to mention the plastic surgery boom) have all contributed to society's overwhelming obsession with covering up. There is something available at almost every corner that is designed to help us look as if something is not there or give the impression that there is more there than what really exists.

The 11th chapter of 2 Samuel describes David's foul attempts to cover up his affair with another man's wife, Bathsheba. David had abused his position as king by having Bathsheba's husband, Uriah, removed from battle and sent home to be with his wife. He thought that by instigating this move, the two would perhaps have sex, therefore making Uriah believe that Bathsheba conceived through their relations. When that plan fell through, David decided upon a more elaborate approach with this particular scheme by making Uriah drunk in order to get him to go home to his wife. After these two unsuccessful attempts to conceal his sin, David descended to an all-time low when he put Uriah in a position to be killed. He told the men who served with Uriah to put him in the forefront of the worst part of the battle and then back off from him when the fighting got fierce. Obviously, there was something going on inside of David that was seriously out of line with the will of God. At the root of it all, behind the position and the prestige was a lying, stealing and conniving murderer. This was the *real* David, the person no one knew existed, so God had to expose it.

WHEN GOD EXPOSES

When God exposes certain behaviors and mannerisms that are contrary to His will for our lives, He does that not just to protect us or keep us from embarrassing ourselves further down the road, but because He loves us and wants us to come into our fullest potential. At this point, there was no way that David would move on to the next level with the stench of adultery and murder lingering over his life. Second Samuel 11:27 says that "this thing David had done displeased the Lord" (NKJV). Yes, even the king had to submit to spiritual authority. Always understand that when we fail to come under spiritual authority because of our hidden things, God is so merciful that He will always send someone to help uncover the real person. More often than not, God exposes the real person through the hearing of the preached Word. Hebrews 4:12 and 13 (NKJV) says,

> ...the word of God is living and powerful, and sharper than any two-edged sword, piercing even to the division of soul and spirit, and of joints and marrow, and is a discerner of the thoughts and intents of the heart: And there is no creature hidden from His sight, but all things are naked and open to the eyes of Him to whom we must give an account.

The Word of God always gets down to the heart of a matter. In David's case, this revelatory word came from a prophet named Nathan. Through a parable that left his sin open and disgraceful in his own sight, David was led to the path of repentance. Second Peter 3:9 (NKJV) says, "The Lord is not slack concerning His promise, as some men count slackness; but is longsuffering toward us, not willing that any should perish, but that all should come to repentance."

Now David may not have even known that these evil characteristics were within him, but God saw what lay beneath David's kingly disposition. Sometimes we don't know what is within us until we're presented with a situation. I believe that these situations are designed to process sinful things out of us.

ACKNOWLEDGEMENT AND REPENTANCE

It is amazing that, prior to David's encounter with the prophet Nathan, he apparently had not felt even an ounce of remorse regarding his behavior. The inherent subtlety of his devious actions suggests that he was totally oblivious to the wickedness that lay beneath. It took God to expose it through His prophet. David was told that because of the hidden things, "the sword will never depart from your house..." (2 Sam. 12:10 NIV). Therefore, Bathsheba's pregnancy was only the first consequence of the callous conduct that landed David in hot water concerning his family, his kingdom, and most importantly, his relationship with God.

Now, the Bible says that Bathsheba bore David a son. According to Nathan's prophecy, this child would surely die. As God's Word prevailed and the child became sick, David began to fast and pray for the healing of the baby; but God wouldn't hear David because of the iniquity he regarded in his heart (Ps. 66:18). God knew exactly what it would take, not only to expose the sin that lay beneath; but also to get David to a place where he would begin to acknowledge his sin. God's exposure and punishment brought David to a place of humility through prayer and fasting. The Bible says that David repented and expressed godly sorrow for his behavior. Here is the Bible's account of David's repentance:

> Have mercy upon me, O God, according to thy loving kindness: according unto the multitude of thy tender mercies blot out my transgressions. Wash me thoroughly from mine iniquity, and cleanse me from my sin. For I acknowledge my transgressions: and my sin is ever before me (Ps. 51:1-3).

> Behold, thou desireth truth in the inward parts: and in the hidden part thou shall make me to know wisdom (Ps. 51:6).

First John 1:9 (NKJV) says, "If we confess our sins, He is faithful and just to forgive us our sins and to cleanse us from all unrighteousness." No matter how great the sin, God is still ready and willing to forgive. If you are reading this message, chances are that God has already begun to expose those things within your heart that are not pleasing to Him. Now it is up to you to acknowledge the Spirit of the Lord's call and to yield to His voice: "...Today, if you will hear His voice, do not harden your hearts" (Heb. 4:7 NKJV).

THE HEART OF THE MATTER

Like David, there is something that lies beneath in every one of us that is either causing a spiritual problem now or could potentially diminish the great plans that God has in store for us. In Psalm 51, David is actually praying, "Help me to dig out what lies beneath and grant me the wisdom to be delivered from the hidden things." David's plea is a genuine cry for a heart change. Many are praying for a mind change but not for a change of heart, and undoubtedly some have been hiding for so long that they don't even know where to begin.

Have you ever known people who have a hidden agenda behind everything they do? They don't know what a healthy relationship is, nor do they ever seem aware of their own shortcomings. This behavior is often a result of what has been instilled through their upbringing. Childhood traumas and unresolved issues have been known to cause severe behavioral problems that manifest themselves even in adulthood. For instance, people who were abused as children tend to grow up to be abusers. I'm not only referring to physical abuse, but emotional and mental abuse as well. In fact, the wounds of emotional and mental abuse can be much more devastating. Low self-esteem, depression and a defeatist attitude are just a few of the many psychological defects spawned by childhood mistreatment.

Developmental psychologists say that once children reach a certain age, their character is already set. They also assert that no one can change their character. Though there is some truth to both statements, God always has the final say. The power of God can change any behavior. Second Corinthians 5:17 says, "If any man be in Christ, he is a **new creature**: old things are passed away; behold, all things are become **new**."

There are many instances in the Bible that show how a person's behavior was changed. One character that comes to mind is Saul, who would later become the apostle Paul. As a persecutor of the early church, he obviously had serious character flaws; however, after his encounter with Jesus, his behavior changed almost immediately. There were still some things lying beneath, but Jesus dealt with those character flaws and changed his heart. (See Acts 9.)

The Bible doesn't mention much about Paul or David's parents' background, but there were evidently some hidden issues within their family histories that caused a seed of rebellion to override their sense of what was right. One translation of Psalm 51:5 and 6 says, "I've been out of step with you for a long time, in the wrong since before I was born. What you're after is truth from the inside out" (MSG). Even though David was a praise and worship leader, a minstrel, a warrior and a king, he still had to come face to face with the reality that there was something deep within his heart that was not right in the sight of God. He said in Psalm 51:10, "Create in me a clean heart, O God; and renew a right spirit within me."

The cold, hard reality of David's entire dilemma was that his heart was filthy. His request was not for an adjusted heart or for God to repair what had malfunctioned, but it was for God to create something totally new on the inside. A heart and a spirit that were right in the eyes of God was now David's greatest desire. This was God's will for David then, and it is what prompts Him to expose the wickedness that lies within our hearts today. God's goal is always to first get us to see ourselves for what we really are, then to confess our sin in order to cultivate our divine destiny.

Unfortunately, we sometimes magnify the sins of others, exposing their faults as yet another attempt at masking our own. Have you ever met someone who always has to be in control? Or maybe someone who always keeps strife going, never satisfied or willing to come to grips with his/her own issues? These are just a few of the behaviors that typify the flesh's innate guise. But God has a way of allowing His Word to reach our very core; it's "a discerner of the thoughts and intents of the heart." Romans 10:10 says, "For with the heart man believeth unto righteousness; and with the mouth confession is made..." Jesus reminds His disciples, "...For out of the abundance of the heart the mouth speaks" (Matt.12:34 and Luke 6:45 NKJV).

IT'S IN THERE?

For a moment, let's look at God's Word as if it were a metal detector. A metal detector is designed to find things that are hidden in the sand or within an area not visible to the naked eye. There is something built into the metal detector that lets you know there is something similar to what you are looking for in a particular place. It is known to detect both trash and treasure; however, it could miss something. Similarly, the Word of God will *discover* the good yet *uncover* the bad. Unlike the metal detector, it never misses a thing!

A problem only arises because of our sinful nature. The flesh does not want to hear the Word of God because it is the Word that reveals what lies beneath. It is the special instrument that cuts through our façade, detecting envy, malice, hatred, deception, wrong motives, discord, witchcraft, generational curses, abuse and other sinful behaviors. None of these may be your hang-up, but I assure you that there is something in there that God wants to uncover that could quite possibly cause you to forfeit your real purpose and miss your blessing if you don't allow Him to deal with it.

In the sixth and seventh chapters of the Book of Joshua, God gave the children of Israel victory at Jericho and issued explicit instructions to them not to take of the accursed things. After this great victory, the children of Israel presumed that their next battle would be a cinch; however, they were defeated. Joshua 7:5 says that their hearts melted and became like water. Upset about what happened, Joshua and the elders fell upon their faces in prayer, but the Lord stopped Joshua and told him that the people had sinned. They had stolen from God by taking of the accursed things and hiding them among their own stuff. God told Joshua that this was why their enemies had defeated them. In other words, there was something lying beneath that caused a setback for the entire nation. This was a perfect example of how unexposed sin can cause total catastrophe in an entire family, or maybe even in an entire community. As per God's instruction, Joshua called all the families together and told them to check their houses in order to uncover the hidden things.

Finally, a man named Achan confessed that he took clothing, silver and gold, then hid the articles amongst his own things. Joshua was instructed to send messengers to Achan's house to remove the accursed things and destroy what he had stolen, along with everything associated with Achan. Achan and his entire family were stoned and then burned to death as punishment for their disobedience. This seems rather cold and merciless; but God had to demonstrate to His people the severity of the consequences of disobedience, while also letting us know its catastrophic effects. I believe that God's Word has detected something lying beneath; and if not dug up and identified, it will continue to defeat you.

You do not have to live in the shadow of defeat, nor do you have to sit behind a mask of corruption. The great benefits of God's grace extended through the blood of His Son Jesus Christ now prevail and are available to you today. God doesn't want to expose you just to embarrass you, but His desire is that all of us men (and women) would repent so that He can lovingly lead and guide us, based upon our right standing with Him. As the psalmist says, "...We are His people and the sheep of His pasture" (Ps. 100:3). Being the Good Shepherd that He is, His utmost concern is always for the best interest of His sheep.

Please take a moment right now and ask God to uncover *the real you*! No more fake smiles! No more charades! Sincerely allow these words to pluck away at the superficial layers of your heart so that a *new dimension of you* may shine forth. The enemy of your soul doesn't even want you to think about the *new you*; he is perfectly okay with your same old church face, "having a form of godliness, but denying the power there-of." On the contrary, God wants us to allow His amazing power to uncover *the real person* in order to present the *new* person faultless before His throne. If you are still not sure where to begin, try starting with Psalm 139:23 and 24: "Search me, O God, and know my heart: try me, and know my thoughts: And see if there be any wicked way in me, and lead me in the way everlasting."

I implore you to do it today! ⌒C8⌒

The Temptation to Quit
(Jeremiah 20:7-10,11-13,14-18)

❧

PASTOR DANTE D. WRIGHT I

Sweet Home Baptist Church of Round Rock
Round Rock, Texas

On July 4, 1952, on a foggy, shrouded morning, a young woman named Florence Chadwick waded into the water off the coast of Catalina Island. Her sole intention was to be the first woman to swim the 21 miles from Catalina Island to the California coast. Long-distance swimming was not something new to her, for she had been the first woman to swim the English Channel in both directions. However, this day's test was one she had yet to face.

The water was numbing cold, and the fog was so thick that she could hardly see the people in her party. Several times, sharks had to be driven away with gunfire. She swam more than 15 hours before she asked to be taken out of the water. Her trainer encouraged her to swim on because they were so close to the coast; but Florence looked, and all she saw was fog. As a result, she quit, less than one-half mile from her goal. Later she said, "I am not making excuses for myself, but if I could have seen my destination, I might have achieved my goal."

MAN'S DESIRE TO SEE WHAT IS AHEAD

As I ponder this story, I realize that many times we too face the same plight that this swimmer faced. We have no intention of failing or quitting; but because we cannot see what is ahead of us, we just throw in the towel or wave the white flag of surrender and say, "I quit."

If I were to survey the sanctuary, poll the parishioners or check with the crowd, I would discover that somebody—from the pulpit to the pews, or from the front door to the back door—is dealing with the temptation to quit on God. There is good news for you: "Winners never quit and quitters never win."

Jeremiah 20:18 introduces us to the fallen condition of man. In verse 20, we meet the character of this text: Jeremiah, the weeping prophet, who was dealing with the ugly, dark demons of depression. Jeremiah is dealing with the "whys" of life: "Why was I born? Why do I have trouble? Why must I face sorrow?"

It is quite odd that the character of this text is dealing with the temptation to quit. This affirms to us that the temptation to quit is not some new struggle in the faith for the neophyte or the novice, but it is an age-old dilemma.

The Book of Jeremiah is an autobiography of one of Judah's greatest prophets during the nation's darkest days. Jeremiah served as one of God's chosen prophets during the nation's darkest days when Jehoiakim was the king. Idolatry and perverted worship were on the rise, and the people of God wallowed in sin. For 40 years, Jeremiah preached God's Word, but no one came forth to accept the living God as Lord and Savior.

Jeremiah did not get into the preaching profession to wear royal regalia; instead, he was called to lead the people to straighten up and fly right in the sight of the Almighty God. He was best known for his wonderful sermons, with statements such as, "Death and destruction are certain if you do not turn from your wicked ways." This is not "The Diary of a Mad Black Woman," but this is the diary of a mad prophet.

The question must be raised, "How does a child of God overcome the emotional, mental, psychological and physical reality of the temptation to quit?"

WE MUST REFRAIN FROM COMPLAINING

Too often as Christians, we do too much complaining to God instead of praising Him. God has done so many great things in the lives of us as believers; however, when we come to church, we hear such complaints as, "Pastor, it's too hot in this building today," or "Pastor, I do not like the person I am sitting next to today."

Do not be discouraged, however. Some of the greatest heroes of the faith had the problem of complaining. In Numbers 11, for example, Moses cried out, "God, I wish you'd kill me! I cannot lead these people any longer because all they do is grumble and mumble about how good the food was back in Egypt." In 1 Kings 19:4, Elijah, after his confrontation with the prophets on Mt. Carmel, rushed into the wilderness and cried, "God just kill me! I am sick and tired of this business of being your prophet." Even Jesus on the cross cried out, "My God, My God, why have you forsaken Me?"

Within this passage, the prophet Jeremiah has a few complaints he wants to express to the living God. In verse seven, observe what Jeremiah says to God: "Oh Lord, you have deceived me." May I exegete the experience of this text? Jeremiah is mad at God! "Deceived" comes from the Hebrew word *pâta*, which Old Testament scholar Walter Brueggemann interprets as, "harassed, taken advantage of, abused or raped." Also, this word denotes being "enticed, allured or tricked."

Jeremiah feels that the Almighty God has been playing games with him, has tricked him and has turned out to be Benedict Arnold because He did not keep His word. Yet, Jeremiah remembers his calling and commission in verses 5, 7 and 8 of the first chapter:

> Before I formed you in the womb I knew you, and before you were born I consecrated you; I have appointed you a prophet to the nations. But the LORD said to me, "Do not say, 'I am a youth,' because everywhere I send you, you shall go. And all that I command you, you shall speak. Do not be afraid of them, for I am with you to deliver you," declares the LORD.

One scholar has suggested that Jeremiah appears to be saying that he understood his relationship to Yahweh to be similar to a marriage bond, but God had used him up and thrown him to the side. Do any of you feel that God has left you hanging and forgot your e-mail, phone number or address? No, He has not, because in His Holy Word He promises to never leave us nor forsake us.

Jeremiah continues his complaint in verse seven, insisting that God despises him. The word (mocketh) in the last part of this verse denotes the idea of "being laughed at or put to shame." Since people could not understand his message, they laughed at him and used the words of his sermons against him, calling him Magor-Missabib, "Death and Destruction."

Have any of you in God's army ever felt as though God despises you? You have been faithful in serving Him and others, but all people do is continually mock you and your service. The good news of God's gospel is that in spite of you feeling deceived and despised, God will get involved in your dilemma and deliver you from your crisis, your complaining and your calamity.

There's a story about a grandfather who went to visit his daughter and her family. He arrived and was very happy to see them. However, his grandson was acting up a little bit. The rules of the house were, if his grandson misbehaved, he was placed in the playpen. That was the disciplinary action taken by his mother.

The baby continued crying, screaming and yelling. It just bothered the grandfather down to the depths of his soul. The grandfather went and picked the baby up out of the playpen. He held and kissed the baby. His daughter, of course, noticed the baby was no longer crying. She went to investigate and asked her father, "What are you doing?" The grandfather replied, "Oh, the baby was crying so I picked him up and held him." His daughter retorted, "The rule of this house is when I put my baby in the playpen, that is where he stays!" The grandfather backed down and said, "OK," as he put the baby back into the playpen.

The baby continued to cry, but the grandfather never left the room. Instead, he came up with this ingenious plan. He said, "Even though I am not allowed to get the baby out of the playpen, my daughter never said that I could not get in the playpen." I do not know where you are in your life, but remember that God will get you out of your pitiful situation. He will pull you out and place your feet on solid ground.

WE MUST RIDE OUT CRITICISM

According to Malcolm X, "If you do not have critics, you will likely have no success." The prophet Jeremiah's public opinion rating, along with his perception of himself, is at an all-time low. He is engaged in a major battle with his countrymen and his own country. As we examine verses nine and 14-18, we see that the prophet is facing the greatest dilemma of his ministry, and this brings on "the temptation to quit."

Jeremiah had to face the criticism from within himself. Verse 20:9a says, "But if say, 'I will not remember him or speak anymore in his name...' ". In a real sense, Jeremiah is telling God, "You can take this job and shove it!" Jeremiah has come to the awful and frightful conclusion as he dibbles and dabbles with the temptation to quit that he is going to sit down, shut up, put his Bible on the shelf and not preach anymore. Jeremiah takes us even further into his mood of melancholy when he states in verse 14, "Cursed be the day I was born." Instead of saying "Happy Birthday," he was saying,

"Cursed be the day I was born." (The Book of Leviticus states that it was a capital crime to curse either God or one's parents.)

Jeremiah also faced criticism from without. Come travel with me back to biblical antiquity where every day in Jeremiah's ministry, he could have been on the Jerusalem Network Channel being ostracized and criticized by the political pundits, his friends, his family and his foes. Verse 10 is quite disturbing. We see that Jeremiah has no one to turn to, nor does he have anyone to talk to in his darkest moments. His friends and foes were waiting to see him trip, slip and fall. They were calculating, speculating and anticipating the moment that he would give in, give out and give up.

Sometimes God allows us to face criticism, crises and challenges. The purpose for this stress, strain and struggle in our lives is for God to put us on display. God does not put us on display for our glory; God puts us on display for *His* glory.

Recently while shopping, I saw a particular fabric from which I was contemplating having a suit designed. But I really was not totally sold on the fabric. As I discussed the possibility of having the suit designed, I still was not sure how this fabric would look in a suit. The tailor offered a suggestion. He said, "We will help you out. If you will look at the dummy on display, it is dressed in a suit of the same fabric you are considering." The tailor gave the dummy a nicer shirt, and suddenly I could see it. The tailor then added a tie. Again, I could see the complete suit properly displayed.

Sometimes God has to get a dummy and place it in front of the people. He then lets the people see the dummy go through hell and watch how the dummy handles his hell. When the dummy goes through hell, he can testify to them, "If it had not been for the Lord on my side, tell me where I would be."

WE MUST RELY ON CHRIST

Let me start by asking you a rhetorical question, "Have any of you in the household of faith ever relied on anyone besides God? Have you ever trusted in someone or some being besides the Almighty God?" To rely on someone means that you trust in that person.

It is very interesting that the Bible is filled with the concept of "one another." The Bible talks about "one another" several times throughout its pages, such as Romans 15:5; 16:16 and John 13:34. But the Bible never tells us to trust one another. Whenever the word "trust" is used in the Bible, it is referring to God. That is why Proverbs 3:5-6 says, "Trust in the Lord with all your heart and lean not unto your own understanding. In all your ways acknowledge Him and He will make your paths straight."

We can learn in our darkest hour the message in the words of the hymn: "What a friend we have in Jesus/All our sins and griefs to bear. What a privilege to carry, everything to God in prayer." Verses 11 and 12 help us to understand how Jeremiah dealt with the temptation to quit: The disillusioned prophet decided to call on the living God. Dr. Adrian Rodgers once said, "Your spiritual life will never be above your prayer life."

We can learn a lot from the prophet Jeremiah. Perhaps, as a wounded warrior in the household of faith, you have stopped talking to God because of your circumstances. Even in the darkest hours of your life, do not stop praying and talking to God. Jeremiah never stopped talking and praying to God, and his prayers ushered in the Lord's protection. When you rely on God during your trials, troubles and tribulations, He will offer you protection and give you triumph over your trials, troubles and tribulations.

Now, for you football fans, we have embarked upon a new season. One thing to observe about the Dallas Cowboys is this: Their management spent a lot of money during the off-season on players. But initially they did not re-sign Terrell Owens or Marion Barber. The first person they re-signed was Flozell Adams. Big Flozell was 6'7" tall and weighed in at 360 pounds.

The advantage of having Big Flozell is that he plays left tackle well. Whenever Romo throws a touchdown and jumps up and down, he does not run to Terrell Owens. He does not run to the other guy who caught the pass, but he turns around and jumps into the arms of his big left tackle, Flozell Adams.

A right-handed quarterback needs a good left tackle because the left tackle protects his blind side. As Romo goes back to pass, he can see in front of him, he can see to the right side of him; but he cannot see behind him. When the ball is snapped, Big Flozell takes a quick step outward, puts his big arms out, and protects anything coming towards Romo's back side.

In a real sense, Romo has no sense what is going on behind him. This is what God does for us. In front of us, we see troubles. To the right, we see our trials. But behind us, God is working out our triumph because, "Surely goodness and mercy shall follow us all the days of our life" (Ps. 23:6). God has got our back.

As we move on, remember the fallen condition of man in the text found in verse 18. Where there is a fallen condition, there is also grace and a reason for celebration. According to Rev. E. K. Bailey, "Grace is the face God wears when he looks at my faults and failures." Verse 13 demonstrates the grace in the text when Jeremiah said, "Sing to the Lord, praise the Lord, for He has delivered the soul of the needy one from the hand of the evildoers." Marvin Sapp, a Christian songwriter, helps us celebrate the grace in the text. *USA Today* reports that Sapp's album was number one for 39 consecutive weeks.

Sapp's album did not just come about. The simple fact is that not only was it number one on the gospel stations, but it was also number one on the contemporary stations. The lyrics Marvin Sapp sang were words everyone could understand. When Sapp penned these lyrics, he wrote them during a time of deep depression because of his father's death. He said he never intended for the words to become a song. However, there is something about going through hell that God will give you a moment to praise.

Marvin Sapp said that through such a time of deep depression he began to write these words:

> Never would have made it
> I never would have made it without You
> I would have lost it all,
> But now I see,
> You were there for me,
> I'm stronger, I am wiser, I am better, so much better
> When I look back over all You brought me through
> I can see that You were the one I held on to
> And I never, never would have made it without You.

That is what Jesus did on Calvary's cross. The good news for us is, just as Jeremiah and Sapp testified, without God they could not have made it. When dealing with the temptation to quit, remember Jesus and the day when He was on Calvary's cross. He demonstrated His love toward us, and today that is why we can rejoice and celebrate. Now we are stronger, we are wiser and we are better—all because of Him and His determination to resist the temptation to quit.

You Can Burn to the End!
(2 Kings 13:14-21)

DR. JOEL C. GREGORY

Professor of Preaching
George W. Truett Theological Seminary
Baylor University, Waco, Texas
Distinguished Fellow, Georgetown College
Georgetown, Kentucky

I recently attended an exposition at the Metropolitan Museum of Art in New York City to view the works of Nicolas Poussin, the famed French landscape artist who died in 1666. All of his life, he had painted pagan subjects such as Greco-Roman landscapes, temples of idols and other classical culture subjects. But at the end of his life, he got religion and decided to paint the Bible. He produced a series of four paintings representing the seasons of the year which now hang in the Louvre. For Autumn, the subject was the spies carrying the grapes from the Valley of Eschol. For Winter, it was Noah and the flood. Spring was Adam and Eve, and Summer was Ruth and Boaz. As he painted these the final paintings before his death, Poussin said, "The swan sings its sweetest song just before it dies, and I want to imitate the swan." Speaking of those paintings, Chateaubriand said, "Sometimes people of genius do their greatest work just before the end. Often men of genius announce their end through masterpieces: it is their soul that takes wings."

If this be true, the last days of Elisha sing more sweetly than any other. We learn from this passage that you can burn all the way until the end.

SAY SOMETHING THAT EMBODIES YOUR LIFE

Some of you are at the dawn of ministry, and it stretches out before you for decades. Some of you are in the midst of ministry, your life half-spent: Half your life is before you, and half is behind you. Some of you are at the end of your ministry, in the autumn days. But the hermeneutical perspective of this message is to look back from the end of ministry and ask, "Will I burn all the way to the end?" First of all, I want you to see that if you burn all the way to the end, you will say something that embodies you.

Elisha, this old prophet, is 90 years old. Lying in his death chamber, he has been off the scene for 50 years. After a robust burst of miraculous activity in his early days, he disappears. Five decades before in a blaze of supernatural days, he turned sour water sweet, replenished the widow's oil, raised the Shunammite's son, purified a pot of stew when there was death in the pot, healed Naaman's leprosy, floated an ax head, saw chariots of fire—and then he was gone. He blazed like a meteor, and then it went quiet. In his early days, Elisha performed miracles like Roman candles, one after the other; but now it is quiet.

Ministers, every day will not be a day when ax heads float. Every day of ministry cannot feature one miracle after another. Ministry is not breathless excitement on a daily basis, and you will be disappointed if you think so. Yes, there will be days when ax heads float and chariots of fire burn, but there will be more days that they do not. Like Elisha's ministry for 50 years, most of our days will be quiet and unnoticed, in the shadows, while we faithfully do the will of God. Even our Lord Jesus Christ said that "the kingdom of God comes without observation."

Now we find Elisha with the death glaze over his eyes, the death sweat on his brow and the rattle in his throat; but he's going to burn to the end. Even though he is 90 years old, he is still ministering—still faithful and fiery. Fred Craddock, the famous homiletician, said that when he was a young preacher, he thought he would write one big check for some dramatic moment or some Olympian deed of ministry. But he found out that after 50 years you don't write one big check. You write a whole lot of little checks—$1.87 here, 97 cents there, $2.50 there—that add up to a lot. In a lifetime of faithfulness, you can always burn for God.

But Joash, the sorry king from a sorry family, got news that Elisha was about to die; so he brought his sorry self down to Gilgal by the fords of the Jordan to see this national icon. Joash, who ruled from about 835-796 B.C. as the 8th ruler after David, respected the legend and the life of the old preacher, the man on whom Elijah's mantle fell. The day that Joash went to see Elisha was a national day filled with significance, such as July 4, 1826, when, incredibly, John Adams and Thomas Jefferson died on the same 4th of July, 50 years to the day after the signing of the Declaration of Independence. Likewise, this was not a day to be missed—when Elisha took his leave.

Joash did not come in and ask Elisha how he was feeling or if he could do something for him. Instead, the king burst into Elisha's sickroom with a cry of respect and affection: "Oh, my father, my father, the chariots of Israel and its horsemen." Isn't that a strange thing to say on a hospital visit? But do you know why he said that? He said those words because they embodied the very life of Elisha. In the same way, you need to minister in such a way that when you say something, that embodies you.

It's interesting that the people we know just by their initials said something that embodied them for all time. When FDR was having his portrait painted at Warm Springs, Georgia, but was stricken at noon, if we were standing over his recumbent form, we might have said, "We have nothing to fear but fear itself." If we were standing over JFK's body at Parkland Hospital in Dallas on that fateful day of November 22, 1963, we would have said, "Ask not what your country can do for you; ask what you can do for your country." If we had been there on that motel balcony in Memphis that day in 1968 when MLK was assassinated, we would have cried, "I have a dream." If we were visiting Sagamore Hill, Long Island, that day in 1919 when TR left us, we would have observed, "It is not the critic that counts but the man in the arena."

Likewise, a single statement stamped the life of Elisha for all time. He was noted and quoted, marked and remarked, for making that statement which embodied his life. You find it in 2 Kings 2:12. When Elisha absolutely refused to leave the side of Elijah his mentor, he went where other prophets would not go and saw what other prophets could not see—the chariot of fire that translated his mentor. There he cried his famous cry, "My father, my father, the chariot of Israel and its horsemen." Yet again, this saying stamped the circumstances of Elisha. When the Syrian army surrounded the defenseless city of Dothan, Elisha's servant quivered with terror. In 2 Kings 6:17 (NKJV), Elisha prayed, " 'Lord, I pray, open his eyes that he may see.' And the Lord opened the eyes of the young man, and he saw. And behold, the mountain was full of horses and chariots of fire all around Elisha." The chariots of fire, again. The cavalry of Israel, again.

When the king burst into his final chamber, the king could not help but cry out these very words that embodied the life and ministry of Elisha. Even the reprobate, apostate, sorry, pusillanimous slacker was forced to cry out the very words that marked the life of the man of God. Elisha said these words at critical times, and everyone remembered them. Elisha cried these words at a critical place when he saw what others did not see and could say what others could not say. Because he had gone where others had not gone, he had seen what others had not seen; therefore, he could say what others had not said. Joash had never seen chariots of fire, but Elisha had. Now Joash, this unworthy king, had made a trip to say something that Elisha said, even though he had not seen what Elisha had seen. Elisha made the eternal world real, even to this sorry slacker of a king.

And this is the call of every ministering person. Oh, that you might see something so real about God in your lifetime that you can say what you have seen, and others who have not seen it can at least say that you said it. That is what ministry can be at its best. Here you are in the pulpit, and there's a man sitting in the pew who has had this mind-numbing sense of having to do something again and again. He has garnered no recognition. He works in a line at the factory or digs holes in a field. He can't look up and see chariots of fire. But on Sunday, because you have seen something, you can say it. Here is the single mother burdened with children, two jobs and debts. No, she does not have time to see chariots of fire during the week, but because you have seen them; you can talk about them to her on Sunday. Even though she cannot see them, she can say something about them because you saw them. Here is a man wasting away in his last days, devoured by a disease that is taking his life. There are tubes and screens, along with hisses and beeps, to tell him that his life is ebbing away. In his terror of the other side, he cannot look up and see chariots of fire; but you can see them and thus tell him that one is coming for him. God, help us to see and say something that will embody us.

There are those who will be remembered for one thing they said. Einstein: $E=mc^2$. Louis XIV: L'etat c'est moi (I am the state). Descartes: *Cogito ergo sum* (I think, therefore I am). In your ministry, let something that you have said embody you.

You may say that you're not Elisha, so you can't speak to all the ages. Don't try to speak to the ages, but say something that will be remembered for a while. It may not be for all of history, but let it be for a while. It may not be for a multitude, but let it be for a few folks. It may not be for the ages, but let it be for a while. It may not be for everybody, but let it be for somebody.

Perhaps we should say less, see more and listen more. An actual university-based study shows that the average woman speaks 8,805 words per day and the average male 6,073. We would do well, as people of God, that just as Elisha was absent and then present, so our presence needs to grow out of our absence. The preacher who is available all the time is not worth anything when he is available. We do not always have to be there. It is even better to let our speaking grow out of our silence. We talk too much when we have seen too little.

Elisha had not said anything in 50 years. When he did finally speak, what he spoke embodied who he was for all time. The best proof of that is that we are here 2,800 years later, talking about what he said. It is better to see and say "chariots of fire" when you have really seen something than to drone on for decades about things that mean nothing and change nothing because we have seen nothing.

DO SOMETHING THAT OUTLASTS YOU

In that chamber with the sweat of death on his brow, the glaze of death on his eyes and the rattle of death in his throat, this old prophet does a surprising thing. Wasting no time, he gives orders to the young king: "Take your bow and some arrows. Put your hand on the bow. Open the east window and shoot the arrow of YAHWEH's deliverance and the arrow of deliverance from Syria."

This astonishing scene marks the last moments of the prophet. The virile hands of the young king stretch the bow and aim the arrow. The 90-

year-old prophet places his icy fingers on the hands of the robust, young king. The mentor says to his mentee, "Open the window and shoot an arrow to the future, and God will guide it to the future." The future depended on the defeat of the Syrian empire. This old prophet rose from his deathbed, put his hands on the king's hands, and cried, "Shoot!" When the king shoots one arrow in the direction of Syria, out of the east window, the prophet cries out a word of power: "The arrow of the victory of YAHWEH." I want you to understand that you can shoot an arrow into the future and do something that outlasts you. Right now, you can do something that inaugurates and predicts the future.

This kind of act belongs to that remarkable set of acts in the Old Testament that both predicted and inaugurated what God was about to do. When Aaron and Hur held up the hands of Moses in the battle against Amalek in Exodus 17, that act both predicted and inaugurated the victory that God was about to give them. Remember when the Lord told Joshua, "Stretch out the spear that is in your hand toward Ai, for I will give it into your hand" (Josh. 8)? In a small way, Joshua did something that God was about to do in a big way. When Joshua did that very thing, God predicted and inaugurated the defeat of Ai. Do you remember when Jeremiah took members of the ministerial alliance and the city council of Jerusalem out to the Valley of the Son of Hinnom and broke an earthen jar in front of them (Jer. 19)? By doing this, he announced that God would break the city if the people did not repent, and the breaking of the jar predicted and inaugurated what He was about to do.

You too can predict something and do something that will outlast you. The old prophet placed his gnarled knuckles on the sinewy hands of the young king and shot an arrow into the future. He acted in the present in such a way that predicted and inaugurated the future. He gave the king an object lesson, a miniature demonstration in the present of what God could do in the future in a larger, fuller way. Similarly, you can shoot an arrow into the future that will predict and inaugurate something much larger that will outlast you.

Whenever God guides an arrow, it unerringly finds its mark. In Homer's *Iliad*, Apollo takes the form of Paris and shoots Achilles in the heel in the decisive battle—the arrow guided unerringly by the god himself. In 1 Kings 22:34, when God had said that Ahab had to go, what happened? A certain man at Ramoth-Gilead shot an arrow at random, and it found its way into the crack in the very joints of the armor of Ahab. When God guides an arrow into the future, that arrow will inevitably find its mark every time.

You can do something that outlasts you. Do not be content to preach, pastor and minister and just disappear. Shoot an arrow into the future, and then God will guide it. Alfred North Whitehead, a mathematician and philosopher, said it well: "A wise man is a man who plants shade trees whose shade he knows that he will never sit under."

When I was a lad, I went with my paternal grandfather Albert Gregory to visit his sister-in-law, my maiden aunt Beulah Hornback. Albert lived to be 90, and Beulah lived to be 103. They were both nearly deaf, so their conversations consisted of screams at one another. I remember one conversation vividly from my boyhood:

> Albert said, "Beulah, I am planting a peach orchard."
> Beulah said, "Albert, you old fool. You will never eat those peaches."
> Albert replied, "I know, but someone will."

Today, five decades later, I drive by a sandy strip of land in Jack County, and there's that peach orchard because "somebody did." He planted a peach orchard and never ate the peaches, but those trees lived and others ate the fruit.

Do something that outlasts you. Shoot an arrow into the future, and let God guide it. Live for more than the narrow confines of today's calendar.

Just like Elisha, as a mentor, put your hands on some young mentee. Tell him when to draw the bow, tell him when to shoot and predict that what he does in a small part today will be great tomorrow. Oh, the difference that is made when someone will shoot an arrow into the future.

I don't know what it will be for you. It may be serving as a mentor to a mentee. It may be building a charter school or helping students by sponsoring a scholarship. It may be building a mission in Kenya or Ghana. Whatever it may be, shoot an arrow into the future. Say, "I want to shoot something into the future that will outlast me."

I have the privilege of being on the faculty at my *alma mater*, Baylor University. Sometimes I walk around that campus at night, and my mind goes back to 1841, when Texas was not even a state. A group of 35 delegates from the Union Baptist Association got together by the San Jacinto River, where the monument was later built, to form a Baptist university. That looked crazy at the time because the Baptists didn't have two dimes to rub together. Also, there probably weren't three Baptists in the whole republic who had a college degree. They accepted the suggestion of Reverend William Milton Tryon and District Judge R.E.B. Baylor to establish a Baptist university in Texas. The Texas

Baptist Education Society then petitioned the Congress of the Republic of Texas to charter a Baptist university in the fall of 1844. Republic President Anson Jones signed the Act of Congress on Feb. 1, 1845, officially establishing Baylor University. Reverend James Huckins, the first Baptist missionary to Texas, was Baylor's first full-time fund-raiser and the third founding father of the university.

Now, 163 years later, as I walk around the 750-acre campus and look at the 14,000 students, the 800 faculty, the 1,500 staff members and the $330-million annual budget, I think of the tens of thousands of ministers and missionaries who have gone out into the world in the name of Jesus, and I thank God that, when there was nothing, they still shot an arrow into the future.

Don't ever doubt that a small thing you do right now can hit a big target. Shoot an arrow into the future and God will guide it. One woman who refused to give up her seat on a bus changed the course of this nation forever. You too can shoot an arrow into the future.

IGNITE SOMETHING THAT BURNS IN YOU

After Joash fired the arrow from his bow, Elisha laid back down with the death sweat on his brow and the death rattle in his throat. Elisha had taken his hands off of the young king. There comes a time when every mentor has to take his hands off of his mentee, if he's a real mentor. And now, Elisha says to the king from his couch, "You shoot!" He expects the king to fire off every arrow in his quiver; but this pusillanimous, lily-livered, spineless, sorry slacker—at the moment of his own destiny—decides to be a conservator of arrows.

Shakespeare said in *Julius Caesar* through the mouth of Brutus before the decisive Battle of Philiippi on which the fate of the Roman Empire would rest:

> There is a tide in the affairs of men,
> Which, taken at the flood, leads on to fortune;
> Omitted, all the voyage of their life
> Is bound in shallows and in miseries.
> On such a full sea are we now afloat;
> And we must take the current when it serves,
> Or lose our ventures.
> —*Julius Caesar*, Act 4, Scene 3

This scene marks Joash's opportunity to turn the floodtide at the crest. That is why the dying prophet is reenergized and burns with life in his last hours. He orders the king to take all of the arrows out of his quiver and to strike the ground with them, which means to shoot the arrows until they stick in the ground. In verse 17, he underscores that Joash should do this utterly, completely, totally, energetically and enthusiastically.

In response, the king shot only three arrows and then stopped. Elisha, full of the anointing of God, was furious with him. Elisha told him that he could have struck five or six times because of the number of arrows in his quiver and ignited something that would have burned forever. The vacillating, pusillanimous, spineless king, however, acted without vision, expectation or hope. Because of what Joash had not done in the present, he limited what God would do in the future. Elisha saw in miniature the large canvas of the future. If the king had struck the ground five or six times, he would have utterly defeated Syria.

There are moments to be seized in the present; and if they are not seized, you will spend the rest of your life regretting that you did not seize them. There are times in our lives when we must empty the quiver, because if we don't the tide will go out. When the tide goes out, it doesn't matter if you're an emperor or a king, you can no more call it back than you can stand at the edge of winter and call back the autumn.

Joash thought he would do only enough to humor the old man. He saw no point in giving himself radically to the words of the prophet. He had come to honor him but not to catch his spirit. Here is the sadness of it, then and now. Joash could have been another Elisha. Just as the spirit of Elijah had fallen on Elisha, the spirit of Elisha at that moment could have fallen on Joash. Had Joash had any spiritual sense, he would have begged Elisha, "Give me a double portion." He stood at a crucial point in history, but he missed his moment. He missed the tide.

Jesus once said to the Pharisees, "Hypocrites! You know how to discern the face of the sky, but you cannot discern the signs of the times" (Matt. 16:3 NKJV). We are realizing more and more that we are living in critical times when we must seize the moment. Right now, everything in our nation's history is about to turn on its hinges, and we need to be ready to empty the quiver and shoot arrows into the future!

Many of us are like the sailor portrayed in a story told by Reinhold Niebuhr, the famous pastor from Detroit and professor of ethics at Union Theological Seminary who influences us to this very day. Niebuhr told the story of a flatland man from an inland state who, all of his life, had dreamed of working on a tall-masted ship. He had never seen the sea, so he rode the rails from that inland state to a port city and enlisted on a ship.

On the third day out to sea, the captain told him to climb the mast and assume the watch from the crow's nest. Halfway up, he froze because he had never been that high up in his life. He had acrophobia, the fear of heights. But when he looked down at the deck, he saw the seasoned sailors ridiculing him because of his fear, so he froze. He neither went up or down; he simply held onto the mast, neither taking his destiny nor refusing it. That is the very epitome of Joash, but let it not be the epitome of us. Let us shoot an arrow into the future and empty our quiver.

I have had the privilege of conducting a series of interviews for Baylor University with Dr. Gardner C. Taylor in the living room of his home in Raleigh-Durham. At first, I was amazed with the content, but then I was amazed with the man. At 90 years of age, there is not anything about him that indicates an ounce of retreat. His eyes are blazing. His mind is full. His will is espousing causes. He was gesturing in the air and sitting on the edge of his chair because something God ignited in him still burns.

It's sad to see preachers and prophets of God burn out before their time of ministry is over. At the end of their lives, all they have are empty dreams, empty eyes and empty hearts. Instead, ignite something in you that will live to the end. You will either be a Joash and miss your moment, or you will be an Elisha and burn all of the way to the end.

Robert Forman Horton served the same parish in Hampstead, England, for 50 years. He gave the Lyman Beecher Lectures on preaching at Yale in 1892. He burned brightly at the same place for 50 years and went out with the same passion that he went in with.

The last entry in his diary was dated March 29, 1934: "United Communion. Eve of the Passion." For that communion he had prepared his message, but he was not destined to share it with the living. Exactly 50 years earlier (March 30, 1884), Robert Horton had written to his sister: "I should like to work up to the last day of my life, and if I might choose, I would die either on leaving my pulpit, or from a disease caught at the bedside of some poor soul to whom I was ministering." His wish was fulfilled. On the very last Sunday of his life he was preaching. To the sick in soul or body he had never ceased to minister, and he lovingly ministered on the day before his death.

In 1917 Theodore Roosevelt was 58 years old, blind in one eye, crippled and overweight. Yet he went hat in hand to his nemesis, President Woodrow Wilson, and begged him to let him gather again a regiment of Rough Riders, just as he had 20 years before at the Battle of San Juan Hill. He wanted to take the regiment to the very thick of the battle in Europe and ride out in a blaze of glory. He had a fire within his soul to the end. On a higher, holier and heavier level it is within the grace of God for each of us that we burn for Him until the end.

ENLIVEN SOMEBODY THAT TOUCHES YOU BEYOND THE END

Verse 30 describes the only posthumous miracle of the Bible at a different time and place, two years later. Elisha has gone to be with his mentor and his God. As his soul has gone to the bosom of Father Abraham, his bones have turned to dust, somewhere near Gilgal at the fords of the Jordan.

A group of his Hebrew brothers were conducting a funeral for one of their own. They had to finish their burial arrangements all in the same day because of the Mediterranean heat. In the middle of their funeral service, they spotted marauding Moabite guerrilla fighters crossing the Jordan to invade Israel. All of a sudden, they were more interested in getting rid of the corpse than staying for the funeral or they were going to be as dead as their brother. At random they removed the top of a rock tomb and dropped their brother into it. They did not know whose tomb they had opened. The very moment their departed brother's corpse touched the bones of Elisha, he sprang back to life. Sirach further says that he started prophesying the moment he came back to life. As a living man, Elisha had placed eye on eye, hand on hand and heart on heart of the dead boy of the Shunnamite widow. There was so much life in this prophet that even when he was dead, something that touched him was brought back to life.

Let there be so much life about you and your ministry that when your life is over, any contact with anything about you will give life. Somebody should touch something about you, and it should come back to life. The minister has more opportunities for that than anyone else. No doctor, politician, lawyer, accountant or anyone else has the same opportunity. Those people you touch will touch others, in an endless succession of spiritual life.

There are those who take life, even after they go. You can name them: Saddam, Stalin and Hitler. Their nefarious activities have spawned hate and death to this day. Wouldn't you rather be somebody who breathes new life into people even though you're gone?

When C.H. Spurgeon died, he was buried in West Norwood Cemetery, south of the Thames in London. Recently I took 40 ministers to visit the site of his tomb. It is in a cemetery of the most notable persons in Victorian England, including the personal physician of Queen Victoria and the Doulton family of Royal Doulton china fame. Yet we were there for none of those. There is one tomb that is visited by thousands. They pray. They praise. They laugh. They cry. It is the tomb of the great preacher. As we stood there, we all sang, "When We All Get to Heaven." We prayed, and we thanked God, and we left uplifted. Why would 40 ministers from across an ocean pay for a bus to take them to a remote cemetery in a huge city? Because from beyond his own life C. H. Spurgeon still touches the world.

I have an original oil painting of Spurgeon on the wall of my study in Fort Worth and a hand-corrected manuscript by him. Sometimes in the middle of the night, I will simply look at the picture or the manuscript, and these 116 years later his life still pours into my life. Subsequently, I want to be better consecrated and more dedicated to the Lord.

But we are not to worship Elisha. There came one greater than Elijah or Elisha:

- Elisha said something that embodied him, but Jesus embodied everything that he said.
- Elisha did something that outlasted him, but Jesus outlasted everything that he did.
- Elisha ignited something that burned in him, but Jesus burned everything before there was any fire.
- Elisha enlivened somebody who touched him, but Jesus enlivened everything before it existed.

Someday they will do with me what they did to that anonymous Hebrew: Put me in the ground. William Saroyan, the short-story writer, said that he knew everybody died; but in his case, he thought they would make an exception. There will be no exceptions except those on earth when the trumpet sounds and the archangels shouts.

They will not have to throw me into an unknown tomb. I know where it is. It will be Plot 29, Oaklawn Section, Greenwood Cemetery, Fort Worth, Texas. You can take your time. They will put me in a box, put that box in a box, put that in the ground and go back to the church and eat potato salad. You can take your time.

But here's where the story's really different. They're not going to have to throw me on anybody's bones for me to live again, because when they came to the tomb that Easter Sunday morning, there weren't any bones around Him. Because of that, you can say something that embodies you, do something that outlasts you, ignite something that burns in you and leave something that gives life to others until your race is run and your day is done and your crown is won. Then you shall stand in glory forever with one greater than Elijah, Elisha or any of his best predecessors or followers. Would you not wish to burn for Him, live for Him, serve for Him, die for Him, awake in glory with Him and forever praise Him?

Edgar Dewitt Jones, *The Royalty of the Pulpit* (New York: Harper & Brothers Publishers, 1951), 63.